To Defy The Odds

To Defy The Odds

An Autobiography

Phyllis Kaminsky

PHYLLIS KAMINSKY

ISBN-13: 9781537682730
ISBN-10: 1537682733

THIS BOOK IS DEDICATED TO MY CHILDREN, DAVID AND GLENN
MY STEPCHILDREN, SHERRY, LOUIS, JAY, AND PHILLIP
MY STEP-GRANDCHILDREN, JOSH, CARA, MORGAN, JAMIE, HALEY,
ASHLEY,
JUSTIN, AND HANNAH
MY STEP-GREAT-GRANDCHILD, CARTER
AND MY GRANDDAUGHTER, BELLA

Contents

Preface #1 · ix
Preface #2 · xiii
Introduction · xvii

Let Us Begin · 1
It's a Long Way to Tipperary · 5
Alone on a Big Ship · 12
The Age of the Ugly American · 18
The New York Rat Race · 24
Monte-Carlo or Bust · 29
Starting Over Again · 40
Steeltown Usa · 46
The Jerusalem Women's Seminar · 52
The Political Bug · 62
That Was The Campaign; This Is The White House · · · · · · · · · 65
The Disunited Nations · 76
The Fall of the Wall · 91
Move Over Guys - Up, Up and Away · · · · · · · · · · · · · · · · · · · 100
An Unlikely Duo · 113
When the Voices of Women are Heard · · · · · · · · · · · · · · · · · · 128
A Love Affair · 135
Like Father Like Son · 141
Here Comes the Sun · 146
Reflections · 155

Phyllis Kaminsky Timeline· 175
Phyllis Levitt Hacin Kaminsky Family Tree· · · · · · · · · · · · · · · · · 179
End Note Halifax Where It All Began · · · · · · · · · · · · · · · · · · 181
Special Acknowledgment· 183
Acknowledgments · 185

Preface #1
GLENN KAMINSKY

I knew pretty early on that my mom was a little different from most of the others. I was in third grade at the Jewish day school in Rockville, Maryland. It was a nice spring day, as I recall, but a little crisp and cool. My mom, as had often been the case, had gotten up pretty early that day to get into work for an early meeting. Me? I'd gotten a pretty good nap in on the bus ride to school, after I made a few trades of my baseball cards or Garbage Pail Kids stickers. I think we spent a little time on the multiplication tables. Recess finally came, and I heard some friends call me over to the monkey bars. There was some laughing, maybe a dare or two, and…the next thing I remember, to the shock and awe of a not insignificant crowd of onlooking youth and teachers, two large men in dark suits were loading me into a large black Lincoln town car with US government license plates. That was when the legend began to grow. Not my legend…hers.

Yes, getting the United States Secret Service to take me to the hospital with a broken wrist was a good way to impress my buddies. To this day, several of them still refer to my mom as "the president." (Alas, as you'll soon find out, she was born in Canada and sadly was never able to run.) When she met me shortly thereafter at the hospital and became the first one to see me with my cast on, I probably told her I wanted to ride home with the agents. I was that kind of kid.

My mom's story is a classic tale of working hard, overcoming challenges and stereotypes, and striving to make a difference in a world where so many people just take the easy way out. I am so glad that she decided to dedicate the time and effort to, in her nonnative tongue, share with us, her family and friends, the stories and firsthand accounts of all the history that she has made. This book is undoubtedly a who's who of the last century and this century as well—sports legends, political and military leaders here and abroad, socialites, celebrities, and many, many people that my mom has encountered and mentored along the way. Including me.

Anyone can write a book, especially an autobiography. But not everyone has the life experience to warrant the effort. My mom definitely does. She's an outlaw (in Slovenia, I think), but also a cop (as a citizen advisor to the FBI). She's a warrior (flying on air force freighters and riding in Air Force One) but also a lover (maybe even of a few interesting and notable men before she met my dad…gasp). She's a Wolverine (Go Blue!), a pianist, and an interior designer—you know, in her free time. She's not a lawyer, but she's always wished she was. (Anyway, we already have too many lawyers in the family.) She's done more in "retirement" than most people do in their main working years.

Mostly, though, she's a mom and grandma, including to my baby daughter Bella, whose Hebrew name Tzipporah she shares. While I can't wait to read this book myself, even more compelling is the chance to see Bella flip through the pages in a few years and think about all the amazing places my mom has been, people she's known, and things she has achieved. I know Bella will be as amazed and proud as I am.

Yeah, my mom was at the White House for her meeting that spring day. It was probably one of the many, many times she was the only woman in a room filled with generals, pompous politicos, and even a few visionary leaders. She may have had to send the Secret Service to pick me up, but, as she always was when she needed to be, she was there at the hospital ready with a hug and a smile, and there was probably a bowl of homemade chicken soup waiting, or at least some tapioca pudding, a treat I recall enjoying around that time. She is a woman of many talents, many passions, and many remarkable achievements. Nothing was handed to her along the way. Let's find out who, what, how, and when!

With Love,
Glenn Kaminsky
Mother's Day, May 8, 2016

Preface #2

DAVID J. HACIN

Like everyone, I'm often asked by new acquaintances, "So, where are you from?" For me, it's a complicated question that inevitably leads to me recounting, with great color and fanfare, some unusual childhood event or adventure—that invariably somehow always leads back to me telling a story about me and my mother. In other words, these conversations start with "Hello, where are you from?" and end with "Well, yes, my mother is quite extraordinary." The stories I tell about my mother may, depending on the audience, involve a princess or a president, a general or a foreign-policy expert, a prime minister, a best-selling author, a tennis star, a famous mayor, or, most frequently, a wonderful man named Sam who knew, despite all the fancy names and places, what was really most important to my mother and, by extension, to me.

This pattern of conversation has been going on all my life, and it still holds true today.

This begins to explain why I have been looking forward to this book with great anticipation. I have always wanted to know how all the events of my mother's life, many of which were of great historic, political, and cultural significance, connect in her mind and what they all mean to her in retrospect. I have been thinking quite a lot about why my mother's life story was so important to me as I grew up and why, even today, I keep recounting parts of her journey with friends and family. Is it pride in her achievement or just a son's love and admiration for his mother? Well, yes, of course, it's all of that. But eventually I came to learn that I tell my mother's story because I am, in fact, the son of someone very special. My mother is a pioneer, and an adventurer, and a risk-taker, and someone who embraces life and her potential to make a difference. My mother's narrative is an interesting story, not just because it moves between very different worlds, events, and people, but mostly because, in the end, her choices were always about her loyalty and commitment to her family and country and, perhaps most passionately, her heritage. Her story evolves. Like any Jewish mother, my mom wants all of her children and grandchildren to live great lives, and her life story reminds all of us to live life like it means something. Like hers does.

As a little boy and into college, I was on just one part of my mother's extraordinary life journey. When she was the daughter of immigrants to Canada, and then America, Mom's ambition to learn and succeed already suggested a remarkable level of courage and independence for a young woman growing up in the 1950s; her subsequent move to Europe, from where her parents had fled, suggests an early longing for independence and adventure and, certainly, curiosity.

Our part of her story started a few years later in Switzerland of the 1960s, after her brief marriage to my father, a rather dashing Slovene architect and Princeton grad who had settled in Geneva to launch his life and career. After I was born in what I imagine was a rather austere world of expats and financial struggles, my mother, sensing she was on the wrong path and in the wrong place, again showed the courage to upend her life, leave my father (and Europe) with a young son in tow, and travel back to New York to start over. It was the *Mad Men* era, and Manhattan was alive with possibilities for a beautiful young go-getter who had grown up a few miles away in the Bronx—seemingly worlds away from Madison

Avenue and Mayor Lindsay's City Hall. All the while trying to juggle the responsibilities of being a working single mother, Mom made a life for us on the upper East Side; we later moved back to Europe to Monte Carlo at its glamorous height, where we mixed with movie stars and royalty. Eventually, after making another course correction, she brought us back to America again, where she reconsidered her priorities and began to realize her dreams of making a difference by going to work for the United Jewish Appeal (UJA).

My grandparents had to be pleased, and I was spending some time getting to know them and much of the rest of the family. It was there that Mom met Sam, a lawyer who came to a UJA meeting and was struck by my mother like a thunderbolt. Of course, he had to woo both of us—me mostly with Italian food and promises of getting a dog. In 1971, we finally headed out to a rapidly deteriorating city in the leafy mountains of western Pennsylvania, where she had to start all over in the unfamiliar terrain of small-town suburbia. In retrospect, it's much easier to see the fragility of it all, but Johnstown was unknowingly sitting on the precipice of a new global economy with the end of an entire way of life in middle America fast on its heels. The flood literally came, I left for college, and Mom reinvented herself yet again.

In just those few years (and up to my departure for college), my mother grew up as a child of immigrants in Montreal, the Bronx, and Queens; secured a place at the University of Michigan at age seventeen; settled and married in postwar Europe; experienced the glamour and excitement of Manhattan and Monte Carlo; made it as a working woman, mother, and wife; adopted a new family; had a second child, Glenn; and then experienced the collapse of the American Rust Belt firsthand. Whatever the big stories of the day, my mother was somehow living in the middle of them, being both influenced and influencer. It's a remarkable setup for her interest and eventual career in politics and international affairs. This was a journey that had a lot of context.

I am grateful to my mother for taking the time to assemble this important book of her memories so that I will continue to have wonderful stories to tell. And, hopefully, a few new ones too.

Mom, we are so proud of you and lucky to have been along for the ride! Thanks for making a difference!

David J. Hacin
Boston, Massachusetts
July 4, 2016—Independence Day

Introduction

My Hebrew name is Tzipporah, meaning "little bird." In biblical history, Tzipporah was the wife of Moses and mother of his two sons. The Book of Exodus tells us that she saved Moses from great danger during their escape from Egypt. Many believe that without Tzipporah, the Hebrews would have never reached the Land of Canaan—the Promised Land—present-day Israel.

Tzipporah represents a woman who may not have thought her life was making much of a difference to the world but whose quiet strength and conviction greatly influenced other people and historic events. A strong woman is one who is determined to do something that other women may not want to do. If I were asked to summarize my life, I would say I believe I lived up to the ideal of the biblical Tzipporah.

My personal odyssey is exemplified by my early decision to lead and to serve. I followed what I call "the Inspiration Model." I believe to inspire is to lead and to lead is to serve. As a first-generation immigrant in America, I had access to very few resources, financial or otherwise. I was pretty much on my own. Nevertheless, I was lucky enough to live an extraordinary life of substance, glamour, and achievement.

I am the daughter of a Jewish resistance fighter in Lithuania in the 1920s. My parents, especially my father, played a very important role in my life. I admired their strength in the face of adversity and the consistency of their values, and I was fortunate to have their boundless love and support. With that in hand, everything was possible for their little bird.

I'd like to share my journey with you.

Let Us Begin

I was born in Montreal, Canada, of immigrant parents who escaped religious persecution in Poland and Lithuania during the early 1930s. I have only vague recollections of my early childhood in Canada. I remember it was cold and it snowed a lot. We didn't have very much. It was a struggle. We had a big fireplace in our kitchen to keep us warm and a big collie named Lassie to protect us. Nonetheless, there was never a lack of love or optimism.

In 1930 my parents boarded a ship in Danzig, Poland, ostensibly bound for America. Most of their relatives had found refuge in the United States. But in a twist of fate, the ship was diverted to Halifax, Nova Scotia, Canada. My mother had a brother in Montreal. My father had a sister in Montreal. Most of their family members had managed to escape, but some ended up in different places—a very common occurrence in those frantic days when many people were trying to escape from the looming dangers of the Hitler regime in Germany. During my childhood in Montreal, my family was in a holding pattern. We were waiting for World War II to mercifully end so we could "go to America."

In August 1945, after D-Day, the border between Canada and the United States was reopened. We were then able to immigrate to America. One month later, in early September 1945, my family, who had escaped the Holocaust, finally rode a train across the border at Rouses Point, from Canada to the United States—their original destination in 1930.

As a young girl of nine, I could not know what life had in store for me. My parents gave me love and confidence to overcome the obstacles

I would surely face. They were also determined to succeed. They struggled to learn French and then English. I struggled as well. My English was not very good, and I sometimes answered in French in school. The teachers in America were not happy with me. I came home from school in tears. My younger sister, Sharon, and I tried hard to fit in.

Our family found sanctuary in the South Bronx, a part of New York City that was often home to a large number of eastern European Jewish immigrant families at the time. Money was scarce. Family events were joyous and sad at the same time. We were happy to be together. But we also waited anxiously for news of other relatives and friends scattered around the globe who might have survived World War II. We were in America, but we were still unsure of the future. The war was finally over. Let the healing begin.

I was in high school during the 1950s. Sweet-sixteen parties were the rage at the time. For my sixteenth birthday, my parents rented a room in a local church and brought in a few modest refreshments for the celebration. A classmate named Rona Burstein was president of the national Eddie Fisher Fan Club. She promised that Eddie Fisher would come to my sweet-sixteen party and sing for us. Sadly but unsurprisingly, Eddie Fisher couldn't make it. So Rona brought a substitute, a young man who was then an unknown singer named Steve Lawrence. He sang "Poinciana" to a group of swooning teenage girls in 1952 in a small room of a church in Long Island City. Rona went on to become the famed Hollywood gossip columnist after changing her name to Rona Barrett. Steve Lawrence is still singing.

I attended W. C. Bryant High School in Long Island City. I was selected to represent my class on a new television game show called *Tic Tac Dough*. As luck would have it, I woke up that morning with a bad case of the mumps. My face was swollen and puffy, my eyes were red, and I had a fever. I still insisted on going. My mother and I showed up at the studio. I was led to the podium. I was very disoriented, with the bright lights shining in my bloodshot eyes.

The first question from the game show host was, "How many days does it take for the moon to rotate around the sun?" I drew a complete blank on a question that every young girl should know how to answer. I was disqualified and quickly dispatched from the stage. My mother and I returned home to deal with the mumps. I was so ashamed to have failed my classmates. I decided that from then on I would make sure I was better prepared. My mother and I laughed it off, but the event was a lesson learned for me.

As far back as I can remember, I was working at one job or another. I was behind a counter making egg creams and ice-cream sodas in my parents' candy store. Early in the mornings, I assembled the Sunday *New York Times* newspaper for the customers for many years. After school hours during my high-school years, I was an AT&T long distance telephone operator in order to save money for college.

In 1956 I interned at the Department of State, Northeast Asia Division in Washington, DC. In 1957 I welcomed Hungarian refugees at Idlewild Airport while interning as a port receptionist for the US Immigration and Naturalization Service.

I worked at various jobs while making my way through the University of Michigan in Ann Arbor, earning an undergraduate degree in international relations and political science and a minor in foreign languages. I did graduate work at Michigan in Soviet history under Professor James Meisel. Professor Meisel was an influential figure in my life. He inspired me to pursue a career in international relations and foreign policy. In order to save tuition money, I completed my undergraduate work in three and a half years. By doing this, I became something of an outlier, and I did not attend the formal graduation ceremony in June 1957. I received my diploma in the mail a few weeks after leaving campus in January of that year.

I returned to New York in early 1957 to start my professional life. I attended night school at Columbia University, aiming for a master's degree in public law and administration and studying at the School of Russian Studies at Columbia University. I have a good ear for languages. I studied Russian, spoke French, and was an effective communicator.

I easily found positions in New York, first at the Ford Foundation and then at the Foreign Policy Association. I was a young woman in a hurry—a very ambitious young woman, at that. I began my career working with the policy elites of the New York foreign-policy establishment. I began to learn and appreciate the global complexities of policy-making. After six months on the job, I was anxious to see the world and experience it for myself.

I visited Europe in 1958 as part of the postcollege graduation ritual for American graduates. It was during that trip that I met my first husband, an American-educated Slovenian architect, Janez Hacin. I never completed my studies for a master's degree at Columbia. I remained in Europe until 1963.

I left Switzerland in December 1963 and returned home to America a much worldlier and more sophisticated young woman. It was then that I began a life journey during which I met and worked with powerful leaders and celebrities around the world—a world filled with challenge, substance, and fulfillment.

So, let us begin. As Frank Sinatra sang, "I did it my way."

It's a Long Way to Tipperary

It was a cold, wintry day in Montreal in 1942. My mother bundled me up for the weather, and we rode the bus to Quebec City. The Queen of England was visiting to show her support for Canadian soldiers in World War II. Quebec City put on a military parade in her honor. My mother and I had come to see my father, Julius Levitt. He was in the Black Watch Regiment of the Canadian Home Guard. And there he was, marching in his Black Watch plaid kilt and black tam-o'-shanter with a look of pride on his face. A man in the crowd lifted me up onto his shoulders so I could wave to him. My father looked so handsome, so proud, so Scottish. He reveled in pomp and circumstance and loved parades and marching music. He was a traditionalist at heart. In the thirties and forties, he had found a temporary place for himself as part of the British Empire, marching to "It's a Long Way to Tipperary." He told me later that he'd never felt the cold that day.

Although my father looked the part, in fact he was not Scottish. He was born in Wilkomir, Lithuania, a suburb of Kaunas, as Yehudah ben Israel Yoselevitz, the son of a forest ranger. My father was an anti-Nazi resistance fighter—a fervent follower of Vladimir Jabotinsky, a teacher and philosopher in the Crimean region of Russia. Jabotinsky was dedicated to a secular liberal philosophy of Jewish national rights expressed in the national homeland of Palestine. He called it "humanitarian Zionism." His chief contribution to Jewish history was as a proponent and organizer of Jewish self-defense. He invented the concept of a modern Jewish military organization, knowing that Jews would have to defend themselves in their future homeland.

The genius of Jabotinsky lay in the fact that he, more than any other Jewish leader of his time, understood the dynamics of the situation in which European Jewry found itself. He anticipated the danger. He loudly and widely predicted the Holocaust and led the effort for illegal immigration, saving thousands of Jews from certain death. As Prime Minister Netanyahu's father, the noted historian Benzion Netanyahu, said in 1931, "He preached resistance to a people who, for many generations, had lost the capacity and the will to resist." Jabotinsky had a very simple goal: the rescue of as many Jews from Europe as possible. My father took up the call. My father's mentor, Menachem Begin, a disciple of Jabotinsky, would go on to become prime minister of Israel in 1977— the year my father passed away.

My father, having escaped to Canada from his native Lithuania in the early thirties, was also proud to be part of "Free Canada," as he called it. But he never forgot his primary objective: a liberated, strong, and independent Jewish people in their ancient homeland.

My father, Julius, had a forceful, almost magnetic personality. He was broad shouldered and ruggedly handsome. His eyes were a piercing blue. When he entered the room, the first thing you saw was the sparkle in his eyes. His eyes were animated, and they twinkled when he spoke. He was a dapper dresser. He never looked casual or sloppy. His shoes were always highly polished, European style. My father stood erect when he walked. I sensed a slight jaunt, almost a swagger, in his footstep. He knew where he was going. He was lean and well-built with a square jawline. When I was young, he had grown a very neat-looking mustache in Canada. The mustache disappeared when we got to America. He had extraordinarily thick and wavy hair. His two grandsons, David and Glenn, seem to have inherited their grandfather's hair.

My father kept his European dining habits. He chewed his food carefully and slowly and smacked his lips when it was really good. He was very deliberate in his eating habits and almost always cleaned his plate.

His life had been a struggle in the old country, having lost many family members to disease, pogroms, and heartbreak in his hometown of Wilkomir. As an immigrant who spoke little English and no French, he had a hard time finding work in wartime Canada. He eventually found a job as a Hebrew teacher in North Bay, Ontario, during the week. He was only home in Montreal on weekends. He was doing what he knew and loved, but he missed being with his family.

My father enjoyed political discussions and kept very well informed. He was a serious man. He rarely made small talk. His handwriting resembled artistic calligraphy. It was deliberate and forceful, as was his personality. He conveyed a sense of intensity about himself and the world.

On the weekends in Montreal, he was busy meeting with his Zionist buddies from Lithuania and Poland, who, like he was, were former members of a Jewish youth group called Betar, in the old country. In the early 1930s, they reunited in Canada with their dreams of saving Jews still to be fulfilled. They came together regularly to despair and lament the Holocaust, which they knew was in full swing. They continued planning for the future of the Jewish people. They were cogs in the global enterprise of saving Jews, arming Jews, and garnering support for Jewish refugees. They were raising money to buy arms and equipment for those who stood on the frontlines of the battle for Jewish survival. They never gave up.

In September 1945 our family finally immigrated to the United States. My father became known legally as Julius Levitt, courtesy of US citizenship authorities who could not pronounce his real name. Again, life was hard, but we were making progress. My sister, Sharon, had come along in January 1945, and my father had a growing family to support. The United States was more open, and work opportunities were more plentiful. He jumped on one of these opportunities. He became the proud owner of a candy store in Long Island City, a suburb of New York. He was known as "Mr. Chocolate Egg Cream." The hours were long and the work was tedious, but my Dad liked the interaction with "real Americans." His customers were on a first-name basis with him, and he was content to be a small merchant in the heart of a suburban community.

Each time my father bought a new candy store, it provided a step up in our lifestyle. We went from Long Island City to Forest Hills to Scarsdale and finally to Bronxville. Every move was bigger and better. But the work never changed. My mother and I would get up early every Sunday morning to assemble the weekend newspapers. There were sometimes twenty sections of the *New York Times* that needed to be put together, and the whole bundle would sell for one dollar. I loved to work behind the counter making milk shakes and various ice-cream drinks.

Sadly, local candy stores don't exist any longer. They have been replaced by Starbucks, Walgreens, and CVS. But there was an era in the fifties when the local candy store served as the gathering place of the neighborhood. And my Dad, Mr. Chocolate Egg Cream, was in his glory.

My father was really an intellectual and a scholar. The candy stores were the vehicle by which he could educate his two daughters. He accepted reality and did what he had to do to take care of his family. Sadly my father was never able to put his intellect and language skills to good use. He stayed well-informed and active in the causes he believed in and watched his children grow up, free and unafraid. As I grew older, I began to understand and appreciate the sacrifices he made.

My dad never lost his sense of humor through it all. I knew he was crying inside when the immensity of the loss of Jewish life during the Hitler era became apparent at the end of World War II. But at least we were all together in America, and we carried on. I was too young to understand how devastating the news was for my family. When they spoke Yiddish to one another I realize now they were trying to protect me from the horror that was unfolding in the world they left behind. Once in awhile a friend who they assumed was dead would show up at our doorstep – usually in the dead of winter. The tears coupled with the screams of joy were unforgettable. These scenes from my childhood remained with me for a lifetime. My parents were stoic but they were emotionally wounded. During the painful years of the 1940s I was frightened and fearful. My parents kept telling me that when we get to America everything will be better. And it was much better.

At family events my dad frequently attempted humor and laughed heartily at himself. Once when we were celebrating my parents' anniversary on the back patio of our beautiful home in the woods in Johnstown, Sam was filming the scene, and my handsome father was clowning around about how long they had been married. He was whispering sweet nothings in my mother's ears and hugging her. My mom was a little embarrassed. My father kept repeating "45 years is a long time". It was almost like he could not believe that life was good and he was having real fun! He was posing for the camera like he was a stand-up comedian. He had us all laughing until tears came. Even our dog was barking. We were all happy but it was always bittersweet. The past was never far away.

My father worried a lot about his health, although he never complained. He was just happy to be alive and living in America. He had an advanced form of heart disease that required major surgery. His younger brother, Abraham, had died of congenital heart failure earlier in Lithuania. Doctors had not perfected bypass procedures in time to benefit my father. He was deemed a surgical risk patient. We all knew it was only a matter of time. I am thankful he lived to see the birth of his grandsons, David and Glenn. He did not live to see me become a member of the White House staff in 1981.

In the early seventies, my parents made a brief two-year *aliyah* to Israel – immigration to Israel. We encouraged them to go. My father's sister and her family were there. It was a dynamic, growing country they deserved to experience. Jews from around the world were streaming in. As my father said, "They had a place to go now where they would feel safe." He had lived long enough to witness the establishment of the State of Israel. He had seen his dream come true. He now had to see the miracle with his own eyes.

The trouble in Israel began for my father because he needed extensive medical resources wherever he was. The complex bureaucracy of nationalized health care in Israel was stultifying, frustrating, and scary.

Israel started out as a socialist state in 1948, and it would take many years before the country took steps to unburden itself of its founding economic doctrine. My father's tales of the health-care bureaucracy in Israel were legendary. He loved Israel, but he was disillusioned with its nationalized health-care system. It was time to go back to America. My father would have to wait a little longer to see his ultimate dream for Israel come true: the election of Menachem Begin as prime minister in 1977.

My parents were happy in 1971 when I married Sam Kaminsky, a small-town lawyer from Johnstown, Pennsylvania. They visited us often. During the winter it was pretty cold in Johnstown, located in the foothills of the Allegheny Mountains. My father did not mind the cold weather. His coat was always buttoned, and his scarf was always tucked in place. Sometimes he wore a dark woolen cap with a beak. During the summer visits, he wore his little yellow cotton hat that he had brought back from Israel.

In July 1977 Johnstown experienced a disastrous flood at the same time Sam and I had made plans for a trip to New York City. We were planning to attend the first public appearance in America of the newly elected prime minister of Israel, Menachem Begin.

This was a very special occasion for my father, who had been, along with Prime Minister Begin, an acolyte of Vladimir Jabotinsky and a member of Betar. The event took place in the Grand Ballroom of the Waldorf Astoria. The aftermath of the flood prevented Sam from being there. Three-year-old Glenn took Sam's seat at the luncheon next to his grandfather. It was good for him to see and feel his grandfather's happiness.

When Prime Minister Begin ascended the podium to a standing ovation from the cheering crowd of three thousand, my father turned to me and said, "This is the happiest day of my life. I've waited fifty years for this moment." He had tears in his glistening blue eyes. I will carry with me forever the look of sheer joy on my father's face. He lifted his grandson, Glenn, over his head in a sign of triumph for all the world to see.

The following Sunday, after I returned to flood-stricken Johnstown, my parents attended an Israeli concert in White Plains. The crowd stood for the singing of "The Star Spangled Banner," followed by the national anthem of Israel called "Hatikvah". My father sat down and instantly died of a massive heart attack. His work was done. We now had to carry on without him. Thankfully, my parents had spent several weeks with us in Johnstown just prior to the flood and my father's death.

After my father died, I received a personal letter from Prime Minister Begin thanking me for my father's dedication to the State of Israel and for his actions that made it possible. I have saved that letter for all generations so they will better understand his legacy to me and to them. My father taught me how to face adversity and to believe deeply. He never wavered in his beliefs throughout his life. He taught me to be a constant Jew and a responsible American and to never give up. He imbued me with the need to be myself, to know myself, and to be proud of who I am.

I delivered the eulogy at my father's funeral. I said, "This was no ordinary man. This was a man with a dream and a song in his heart that filled his life. The song was Israel. His heart did not stop. It is beating in Israel. His handsome face will forever be with his people and his family that loved him."

I often wonder what he would say about the world situation if he were alive today. I know he would be very angry at and disappointed by the way his beloved Israel is being demonized throughout most of Europe and even in the United States. I think he would have been confident that, in spite of it all, the Jewish people would survive. My father would be out there fighting the good fight and never giving up.

His favorite song was "It's a Long Way to Tipperary. It's a long way to go." I'm sure my father would tell me, "We're not there yet." It's a long way to go…

ALONE ON A BIG SHIP

It was 1929—a year before the Nazi Party would become the second-largest political party in Germany. A young mother, Sarah, and her young daughter, Betty, were finally in Danzig after a harrowing escape from Lvov, Poland, via an international safe corridor. Sarah, my grandmother, bribed local border and customs officials with pieces of silver they had carried with them. The city of Danzig had been declared a "Free City," and she was determined to get there. A Free City at that time was like a no-fly zone in our time. It was a place where refugees could be safe as they awaited further resettlement. My grandmother's older child, Jack, had left earlier and immigrated to Montreal, Canada, with his Polish wife, Anna. Sarah's three other daughters, Freda, Dinah, and Jean, had been able to leave and were in America.

My grandmother was on the run because my grandfather, Levi Shapiro, had been murdered by Polish thugs—shot through the wooden front door of their home. My mother, Betty Shapiro, could never bring herself to talk about that.

Levi was a successful owner of a small sawmill and had done well over the years. The Poles wanted his property and business, so they killed him and took it. That's the way life was for Jews in eastern Europe in the late 1920s and 1930s. Jews lived in fear and uncertainty. Some Jewish families left. But many stayed on in their shtetls and ghettoes.

After my grandfather's killing, my brave grandmother, Sarah, read the handwriting on the wall for Jews in Poland. The Nazis were coming.

The remaining Jews would not be safe. It was time to leave for the promised land: America.

When they reached Danzig, the waiting began. Sarah and her daughter waited patiently for visas to go to America. Before obtaining one, applicants had to receive medical clearance from an American doctor. My mother had been held back for several months because of a chronic eye infection. On January 10, 1930, my mother in her school uniform boarded the ship called the *Lituania* so she could be examined by the onboard American doctor. Her eye infection had cleared. My mother was approved for a visa to America.

Before she could disembark to tell her mother the good news, the large ship, filled with immigrant families headed for a transatlantic voyage to America, started moving out of the port of Danzig. When she realized the ship was making its way out of the crowded harbor, she panicked. My mother had planned to go home and leave on a future sailing with her mother, who already had a visa.

My mother stood at the railing and started screaming to be let off. She appeared to be ready to jump into the water. But there was no turning back. The ship was leaving whether she was ready or not. She was young, under eighteen, and alone on a big ship, without any personal belongings except her schoolbooks. And there was no going back. She was going to America.

A handsome young man on the ship noticed my mother's distress and offered to help her. And help he did. He cared for her and protected her through the grueling, icy twelve-day Atlantic crossing in the middle of winter. The young man was my father. The ship had originally been destined for Ellis Island, but for reasons unknown to me, it ended up in Nova Scotia, Canada. A year later, my parents married in Montreal, Canada, where my sister and I were born.

During the chaotic days of the early 1930s, filled with pogroms and protests throughout central Europe, many Jews left their villages and farms to seek safety and freedom. It was not unusual for immigrant transport ships to change their destination ports. My parents had been wise to leave Europe before it was too late, even if they didn't quite make it to their preferred destination. After my mother had sailed, the authorities notified my grandmother of her departure. She sailed to the United States several weeks later on a ship that did, in fact, arrive at Ellis Island, where she was met by her three other daughters.

Our life in Montreal was not easy, but we made it work. My father found a job out of town and was away during the week. My mother always urged me to eat my spinach and liver because "there were starving people in India." She sewed zippers in hundreds of skirts so I could take piano lessons starting at the age of six.

In her recent book, Peggy Noonan wrote that Margaret Thatcher's mother, Pope John Paul's mother, and Ronald Reagan's mother all worked at home sewing clothes to make money for the family. My mother was in very good company.

We didn't have a car or any of the luxuries in life. But we had a piano. Immigrant Jewish families wanted their children to learn everything, particularly music, math, and English. A piano was considered the stepping stone to success. It was a status symbol. In many English historical dramas, young women also played the piano. It would help them find a worthy and wealthy husband. Jewish families aspired to the same thing.

My mother was always courageous and strong. In 1945, when I was eight years old, my mother and I were on a streetcar in Montreal. My mother was in her ninth month of pregnancy. She started having labor pains. She made me get off the streetcar and walk home. She continued on to the Montreal General Hospital stop and walked into the hospital all by herself to give birth. That's how my sister, Sharon, came into our world.

Many years later, Sharon married and gave birth to Jennifer, my only niece, who now lives with her two children, Levi and Maya, and husband, Chris, in Melbourne, Australia.

My mother always worked. She was a seamstress, a waitress—whatever she had to be to earn enough money to help care for her family. She was a self-sacrificing person who never expected anything to come easy. She always stood at my father's side with her warm and gentle personality.

It was not until September 1945 that my mother would be reunited with her sisters in America. They were eager to help with jobs, money, and love during those difficult first years. In those days immigrant families were very close, sharing their lives and what little they had with each other. My father's health had started to become a source of worry for my mother. He needed constant monitoring and care. For her whole life, my mother loved only the man who rescued her that traumatic day in the port of Danzig. She would be his partner for life.

After my father passed away in 1977, my mother lived a quiet life at her home in Lake Worth, Florida. In many ways she emerged from living in the shadow of my father. She became active in the local chapter of Hadassah and ORT, both Jewish organizations dedicated to caring for, rehabilitating, and educating Jews worldwide. She was a local spokesperson for the movement to free Soviet Jewry. She left me handwritten copies of the many passionate speeches she delivered about the issue. She too had become a fighter for the Jewish people. In a way, my mother picked up where my father had left off. She had watched him over the years and knew how to do it. She finally came into her own and blossomed into a full-fledged activist after his death. I encouraged her to do so. She had so much to offer.

My mother was the epitome of a good person. She was very engaging and loved people. She had many friends, and even though she worked hard, she rarely complained. She was content to raise her two daughters. She was especially close to her grandchildren and was always there for them when needed. They visited her often after she settled in Florida.

My mother endlessly gave love, sustenance, and support to all of us. She was especially close to my second husband, Sam. After one of her visits to us in Johnstown, she sent us a thank you note:Dear Children "It felt good to be a part of your life. Yours and Sam's concern for my well-being and caring for me make me a very lucky mother…All I can do is give you all my love and share my pride at being your mother."

She loved to garden and used to sit for hours watching wildlife shows on television. In Florida she finally was able to plant and cultivate a small garden with a bird feeder. It was her pride and joy. In my mind she was the original environmentalist.

Eventually, my mother moved into a senior-living facility in Deerfield Beach, Florida. She had developed macular degeneration, a condition that clipped her independence and her ability to see the flowers, plants, and birds she loved. Her eyes had always been her weakest link. My sister, Sharon, and her daughter, Jennifer, lived nearby and visited often. I was there as often as I could, flying in from DC several times a year.

On October 24, 1999, Sam and I were at a small private dinner hosted by the Turkish ambassador and his wife in DC. Other guests included General Cevik Bir, deputy chairman of the Turkish General Staff, and General Joe Ralston, deputy chairman of the Joint Chiefs of Staff, and their wives. When we arrived home after the dinner, I learned that my mother had left us, after a long and giving life.

My mother took her love and beautiful smile with her. Life had been a set of constant challenges, but she persevered and met all of them with grace and dignity. My mother lived twenty-two years after the death of my father. She was lonely and incomplete without him, and she missed his spirited companionship. However, she became her own person with her own dreams. I loved and respected her very much. I will always miss her goodness, gentle touch, and winning smile.

My mother had an unfulfilled dream to visit all the US national parks. Sam promised me that someday we would make the trip in her honor. In 2014 my mother's dream came true. We visited Yellowstone, the Grand Tetons, the Black Hills of South Dakota, Mount Rushmore, Mount Crazy Horse, Custer State Park, the Snake River, Rocky Mountain State Park, Deadwood, Cheyenne, Cody, and Jackson Hole.

During that trip, I was very moved by a plaque on one of the walls of the Grand Tetons National Park Museum. It said: "You must search for the loveliness of America; It is not obvious; It is scattered; But when you find it, it touches you and binds you to it like a great secret oath taken in silence." It was written in 1934 by Struthers Burt, a dude rancher from Jackson Hole, Wyoming. The quote reinforced my love for America and my good fortune that my parents were able to be part of this great country in all its beauty and splendor.

THE AGE OF THE UGLY AMERICAN

In May 1958 I became a naturalized American citizen. The naturalization process was relatively simple. It happened at the county courthouse in White Plains, New York, with my parents by my side. I gave up my Canadian citizenship, and my Canadian passport was canceled. I made a pledge of allegiance to the United States and became a full-fledged American.

The year 1958 signaled the start of the era of the "Ugly American." The Vietnam War was in full swing. It was an ugly war played out on the front pages of newspapers around the world. Many of the victims of a US bombing campaign were Vietnamese civilians. World public opinion quickly turned against America. There was widespread anger at the brutality of the conflict. America had lost the high ground, and we were looked upon by many as the Ugly Americans almost everywhere in the world. We were welcomed as tourists and students even though our policies were privately repudiated. The American dollar was still highly valued. But for Americans the Vietnam War was very hard to explain or justify.

In the summer of 1958, my parents gave me a trip to Europe as my college graduation gift. In the late 1950s, Europe was romantic, elegant, optimistic, and welcoming to Americans. Cesare, a handsome Italian, serenaded me on a gondolier in Venice; my Canadian French caused quite a stir in Paris; I refused to get on a bus going to the suburb of Dachau in Munich; I walked through the Anne Frank House in Amsterdam as if in a trance; I witnessed the majesty of the glorious, snow-covered Alps; and I danced the night away on the French Riviera.

While I was dancing on the French Riviera, America was going through a period of great turmoil and upheaval: the failed Bay of Pigs adventure in Cuba; the controversial, bloody war in Vietnam; the rise of the Black Panthers liberation movement; the fight for women's rights launched by Bella Abzug, Gloria Steinem, and others. And an important new constituency, comprising the eighteen-year-olds, was granted the right to vote. Excitement and energy rippled through American society. There was also tension and anxiety. I was still too young and idealistic to understand the changing dynamics of American society in the late fifties and early sixties.

When I arrived in Geneva, Switzerland, in the late summer of 1958, I phoned a young Yugoslav architect, Janez Hacin. I had met him on a blind date a year earlier, when he was studying at Princeton. Caroline Higginbotham, whom I worked with at the Ford Foundation, had introduced me to him. Her boyfriend was Janez's roommate at Princeton. Janez was planning to live in Switzerland after graduation. He was the only member of his family who had chosen to live in the West. Janez told me to give him a call if I came through Geneva during my travels in Europe. I made the phone call that would change my life.

After a whirlwind courtship traveling around Switzerland and Austria, Janez and I were married in a civil ceremony by a French-speaking justice of the peace at the City Hall of Geneva on February 5, 1959.

Janez was born in Slovenia, the smallest republic in former Yugoslavia. He left Slovenia to attend Princeton University on a UNESCO scholarship in the mid-1950s. His father was a diplomat and a banker. His older sister was a Supreme Court judge. His younger sister was married to a top law enforcement official. They were part of the fabric of the Communist society Janez left behind.

Janez's father became gravely ill while he was at Princeton. Janez was unable to return before his father passed away. He told me that after his father's death the family found the acceptance letter from Princeton under the pillow of his father's hospital bed. His father never had the chance to tell Janez how proud he was of his only son. Janez did not return to Slovenia until 1991, when the country threw off Communist rule and declared its independence from Yugoslavia.

Janez was very talented, and he quickly found work at an architecture firm in the Old Town of Geneva. We started our life together in a charming old building with few modern amenities and a steep spiral staircase leading to our small third-floor apartment. We were in love. What did it matter. Three years later we moved to a grand modern apartment in an upscale section of Geneva where many other foreign expatriates lived. Janez was doing well and gaining recognition for his design skills. He bought a dark-green Jaguar XK 150 convertible. We were moving up in the world.

Life in Geneva was difficult and unfulfilling. Geneva is a city that consists of several anomalies—it is a city with several distinct communities living separate lives. First, there are the native well-to-do Swiss executives and bankers and their families. Then there is the international crowd of civil servants who work across the Lake of Geneva for the United Nations and various other organizations, such as the International Labor Organization, World Health Organization, and many more. This group also includes the diplomatic missions to the UN and their staff.

There was also a group of foreign residents involved in international business, most of whom spoke little French and lived in Geneva for varying periods of time. And finally, there was a group comprising blue- and white-collar workers—the normal population of a medium-sized metropolitan city. the different groups rarely interacted, except by accident. The Swiss liked it that way, and they tried very hard to keep it that way. Geneva was socially rigid, unlike the United States, where neighbors interacted with block parties and picnics. I greatly missed the part of American life that was so open and sharing.

Being both American and European, Janez and I were able to cross boundaries. We socialized with some UN officials, as well as some younger Swiss bankers who were friends of Janez's Swiss business partner, Dominique Gampert. Our closest friends were American and foreign expatriates who came and went. Our social life in Geneva was a constant challenge. We did not belong to any of the communities. We were something of a hybrid. We traveled extensively, mostly to ski resorts. Janez was an avid, daredevil skier. After spending a lot of time in ski schools, I gradually picked up my game and learned to hold my own on the slopes.

There was also a dark side to Geneva. In the early sixties, an American named Bernie Cornfeld came to Geneva to set up the Fund of Funds. The Fund was selling mutual funds primarily to Americans stationed abroad, mostly those in the military. In his heyday, Bernie and his jet-setter wheeler-dealer associates moved in and out of Geneva society. In truth they were operating a big financial pyramid scam that was eventually uncovered by Swiss authorities. His illegal activity was particularly offensive because his victims were primarily US servicemen stationed in Europe. Bernie ended up in jail in Geneva for many years. His arrest and jailing put a damper on foreign residents' speculative activities in Switzerland. There was always a feeling that we were being watched by the Swiss police.

There were also the money launderers, the tax evaders, the arms dealers, and the former or present dictators living or hiding out in luxury mansions along the shores of Lake Geneva. They had an entourage of bodyguards wherever they went. And along with the multiple UN agencies came human rights activists, environmentalists and so-called development experts from all over the world.

The Americans tended to hang together. When they ventured out to meet the locals, they encountered curiosity and hostility. The Vietnam War had awakened strong anti-American feelings in Europe. Americans were the outsiders in Europe no matter how hard they tried to integrate. Once in a while, some friends from Serbia, Slovenia, and Bosnia would pass through, and Janez would catch up on news from the old country. Ironically, many years later, after my return to the United States, I became deeply involved, on behalf of the US government, in the events that followed the breakup of the former Yugoslavia.

During my time in Geneva, I worked at the United Nations, Chrysler International, and McKinsey and Company. I delivered my first son,

David, by natural childbirth at the Clinique Bois Gentil, where the staff spoke only French, on July 7, 1961. David Janez Hacin made a huge and happy difference in our lives.

Even with David in our lives, I was becoming more and more homesick for my family and friends. I finally admitted I was lonely. I think Janez was also homesick, but he could not or did not want to return to communist Yugoslavia. However, I had a better option: to return to a free America that had welcomed my parents and their families.

My parents never said anything, but I knew I had broken their hearts with the choices I made. However, they were always strong and supportive. They came to Geneva for a brief visit in 1962 to see their new grandson. They only stayed a few days. Being in Europe reminded my parents of the horrors of World War II. My parents had little love or sentiment for Europe. My father called it the "graveyard of the Jewish people."

November 22, 1963, was a normal work day for me in Geneva. At that time I was a secretarial supervisor at McKinsey and Company, a prestigious international management-consulting company. I briefly heard the news before I left home. President Kennedy had been shot in Dallas. By the time I reached my office, the announcement had come through that the president had died. My grief overwhelmed me. I was inconsolable. I immediately felt the huge distance between Europe and America. I realized at that moment that I had to go home to America. What was I doing in Europe anyway? On that fateful day, I made one of the most anguished and difficult decisions of my life.

After many tears and much heartbreak, I left my life and husband in Geneva a few weeks later. It was time to pick up the pieces of my life in the United States. I packed up my things, bought a ticket on TWA, and flew home with my two-and-a-half-year-old son, David. I had fifty Swiss francs, approximately twenty dollars, in my wallet. The looks on the faces of my welcoming parents at the airport were worth a million times that much. Their brief interlude of sadness and heartbreak was over! I had finally come home after my five-year European interlude.

In 1964 I was young, healthy, and anxious to make a new start. So I joined the rat race, otherwise known as life and love in New York City. I happily rejoined the millions of ugly Americans who were always trying to do the right thing in the world and who always had the best of intentions. Sadly Americans have had little success in being understood and appreciated. But we will keep trying.

Three years later, in 1966, I received a Mexican divorce from the talented, wonderful man I had married in Geneva. Our cultural differences and divided loyalties made it very difficult for our marriage to succeed. Janez remained in Geneva and went on to great success as an architect. He was a European. I was an American. We tried hard, but we could not make it work. We cared deeply about different things. We had vastly different dreams. As my mother said, "The apple had fallen too far from the tree." We both remarried and had children. Our two families remain close and continue to share many happy events.

THE NEW YORK RAT RACE

It was early 1964. I returned to the United States from Geneva as a single mother. Financially stressed and trying to care for a young child, I was determined to make up for lost time. I found it really tough to juggle raising a young child as a single mom, working full-time, and coping with an active social life. I was a playgirl, career woman, and mother all at the same time. My parents were very helpful as I launched into the rat race, a phenomenon that exemplifies most young people's lives in the Big Apple—a constant whirlwind.

David was exceptionally creative. His pleasant personality and easy-going disposition helped him adapt to new situations quickly. He was awarded a full scholarship at the Dalton School, one of the most prestigious private elementary schools in New York City. They recognized David's quick mind and artistic skills when he was very young. He was a gifted and trusting child.

I was going through housekeepers like crazy. It was all part of the New York lifestyle. People moved around constantly and changed jobs frequently. Permanence was not part of the New York playbook. It was a city in motion. We moved three times in the course of six years. I started out as an executive secretary for the senior partner of a prominent New York law firm. A year later I accepted a position as executive assistant to the international vice-president of Grey Advertising, one of the top agencies in the world. The job was fast-paced and glamorous. However, I did not last long at Grey Advertising either. I had bigger plans for myself.

From 1964 until late 1967, I was involved in an ill-fated four-year romantic entanglement with a well-known legal hotshot in New York, Andrew N. Heine. Andy was very handsome, successful, and wealthy—a New York celebrity of sorts. In short, he was a lady-killer. I was easy prey. He was pondering divorce. He was sometimes separated from his wife and sometimes not. He had three young children. After many years of heartbreak and frustration, we ended the relationship. Andy went on to marry two more times and father two more children. I never looked back. I do, however, regret the waste of almost four years of my life in a flawed relationship with an unworthy partner.

During that time the off-Broadway show *The Fantasticks* was a big favorite for many years. The theme song of the show, by Jacques Brel, said, "Try to remember the kind of September when life was so tender, when love was an ember. Without a hurt, a heart is hollow. Try to remember and if you remember then follow, follow." I pined for a while and meditated about what to do next, and by year's end I had moved on. A failed love affair would not hold me back. I was young and undaunted, filled with optimism.

In 1968 I left the life of a New York City playgirl behind me—but only temporarily. Joan Sands, a friend whom I had worked with at the Ford Foundation, was serving as the mayor's director of Special Events. She called me and used six magic words: "I have a job for you." Joan offered me a position as deputy director of the Consular Corps. I was put in charge of outreach to the diplomatic community based in New York and at the United Nations. I jumped at the opportunity to join the administration of Mayor John Lindsay, considered to be a rising star in the Republican Party.

Lindsay was a patrician figure who endeared himself to the citizens of New York by throwing off his elitist background and reaching out to its citizens—all its citizens. He visited minority neighborhoods often, to show his special concern. The Lindsay administration was in many ways a civil rights administration. His made it his priority to improve life for New York's black and Puerto Rican citizens. He spent many years trying to do the almost impossible: bringing progress and positive change to those less fortunate New Yorkers who were having a hard time keeping up with the city's fast-paced way of life. Many neighborhoods were run-down and poorly serviced. The residents were crying out for attention. John Lindsay paid attention and succeeded to some degree, whereas other mayors had not even made the effort.

My immediate boss was Bud Palmer, the famed pioneer of the jump shot in basketball. Bud was commissioner of Public Events. The mayor frequently took his personal staff with him when he made his frequent forays to different New York City neighborhoods. Parts of New York were very tense and hostile to elected officials.

On April 4, 1968, the night Martin Luther King Jr. was assassinated in Memphis, Mayor Lindsay chose his three top political advisors, Dave Garth, Sid Davidoff, and Barry Gottehrer, to accompany him on his famous "walk through the streets of Harlem" at a time when racial tensions were very high. I was never more proud of John Lindsay than on that night. He proved himself to be a hands-on politician. He showed the rest of the country his great courage and dedication. His presence and soothing words that tragic night helped to reassure and calm all New Yorkers. The Harlem residents truly felt that Lindsay was the one politician they could trust and rely on. They understood his determination to make New York City a fairer and better place for all its residents. It would take many decades to do what was necessary. John Lindsay made a good start.

In June 1968 the *New York Times* ran a full-page spread entitled "To Fun City's Girl Fridays, a 12-hour Day Isn't Work, It's Play," bylined by Enid Nemy. The seven women featured in the article were under thirty and working for the mayor. I was one of them. In the article I was quoted as saying, "It's fascinating because this is a people job." We became overnight celebrities. We were invited everywhere, but we didn't have much free time to be party girls. We were busy working for the mayor of Fun City, as he called it.

By chance in April 1968, I was seated next to the consul general of the Principality of Monaco, Mr. Rafael Palmaro. We were at a

Pan-American Day luncheon hosted by the mayor—a glittering annual event held at the Lincoln Center for celebrities and politicians. I could tell that Mr. Palmaro preferred to speak French. I was glad to have an opportunity to show off my French for a couple of hours. At the end of lunch, Mr. Palmaro said in French that he "might have an interesting job opportunity" for me. On the spot he offered me a job as director of Press Relations for the Monte Carlo resort complex owned and operated by the Grimaldi royal family—whose most famous member was the American actress Grace Kelly.

I told Mr. Palmaro that I was very flattered and intrigued by his exciting offer but that I would have to decline. Mayor Lindsay and his team did not yet know that I had made a prior commitment to Bobby Kennedy's presidential campaign. I had already accepted the job of press secretary and spokesperson for the upcoming all-important New York primary in June of 1968—immediately following the California primary, which he was expected to win.

Bobby Kennedy inspired me early on. While I was in Geneva in the early sixties, when he was attorney general, I had written to him and expressed my support. While serving in the Lindsay administration, I had become acquainted with many of the top New York City political leaders. One day while attending an official event, Percy Sutton, Manhattan Borough president, approached me and offered me a job in Bobby's presidential campaign. He had touched my soft spot. I was already a fan of Camelot. I was swept up in the Kennedy mystique. "Don't let it be forgot that once there was a spot for one brief shining moment that was known as Camelot." I accepted right away. I was eager to join my first political campaign. Here I was working for a Republican mayor and joining a Democratic presidential campaign. I saw myself as a bipartisan political operative working both sides of the fence. In the late sixties, politics were kinder and gentler, and I looked forward to serving in a Bobby Kennedy administration.

On June 6, 1968, my world was turned upside down again. Bobby Kennedy was assassinated in Los Angeles. I had reached another defining moment in my life—another Kennedy moment. Our country will never know what we lost that day in June 1968 in the kitchen of a Los Angeles hotel. To me Bobby held out the possibility of being a strong, authentic leader. So did John Lindsay. Bobby Kennedy said, "Some men see things as they are and say, why; I dream things that never were and say, why not." I was a dreamer.

I grieved deeply for a while. After several weeks I called Mr. Palmaro, the consul General of Monaco, and accepted his generous offer to work in Monte Carlo. I resigned my position with the Lindsay administration and started packing. This time I was running away back to Europe. In August 1968, two months later, I flew into the airport in Nice, France, with my seven-year-old son, David, in tow, ready to embark on the next part of my life journey. On to a dazzling life on the French Riviera.

MONTE-CARLO OR BUST

It was late August 1968. Once again, I bundled up my son, David, now seven years old; boarded a plane; and started a new adventure. We were on our way to Europe once again. Nine hours later we arrived at the Nice airport in southern France. A black limousine was waiting for us, and it whisked us to the Hotel Hermitage in Monte Carlo. Our first view of the rocky promontory known as the Principality of Monaco took in the imposing Grimaldi palace, the many yachts in the harbor, and the almost pristine blue Mediterranean Sea. We were in the world's second-smallest country: a jewel-like entity wrapped in luxury, opulence, and fantasy. The views of the Monte Carlo harbor from our apartment took our breath away. David and I were overwhelmed at first sighting of the place that would be our home for the next two years. He was seven when we arrived and would be nine when he returned to the United States in late 1970.

We were quickly thrown into a world where almost everyone spoke French. A few people spoke a little English. My French was pretty good after having lived in Geneva for five years. David had picked up some French during the time he spent visiting his father after our divorce. His French was actually pretty good.

We ventured out in our new surroundings, ready to become citizens of Monaco—"Monagasques," as they were called. I knew almost immediately that Monaco was an idyllic place but also a sort of safe harbor for people who needed a haven for themselves and their money. There were banks everywhere.

Phyllis Kaminsky

I was the only American on the senior staff of the Societe des Bains de Mer (SBM), the entity that owns and operates the Monte Carlo resort and casino for the Grimaldi royal family, headed by Their Serene Highnesses Prince Rainier and Princess Grace. I held the title of director of Press Relations—an important function for a principality that thrived and depended on celebrity status, fancy social events, and foreign tourists. The SBM was headed by Wilfred de Groote, a suave Dutchman with social skills extraordinaire. His deputies included a Monagasque, Andre Rolfo-Fontana, a product of his close-knit upbringing and family connections, and a Frenchman, Guy Levrier, who was a consummate advertising and marketing bureaucrat. Nadia Lacoste, who was based in Paris, was the tourism director and a long-time confidante of the Grimaldi family.

Nadia was an American who had become a complete Francophile. I was never able to break through to her even though we shared a common heritage. I met with her several times, but we never became friends. For her I was the newcomer and someone who probably wouldn't be around for very long. Or she may have felt I was infringing on her territory. I would have appreciated her wise counsel. Too bad. I would have liked to know her better and learn some tricks of the trade from her.

I was young, single, and sought after, and I made many new friends very quickly. I decided that Monte Carlo was not the right place for my seven-year-old son to attend school. The world of gambling, galas, and glitz was not the right environment for a young child. With help from my dear friend Josephine (Josie) Miller, we found a nice private home and French school for him in Saint-Jean-Cap-Ferrat, across the border in France—about a twenty-minute drive from Monaco. We would spend the weekends together, and I would frequently have dinner with him in the quaint French fishing village he would live in for the next two years. In the end, I put thousands of miles on my little red Fiat convertible, taking in the beautiful scenery on my way to and from Saint-Jean. The drive was always well worth it. David was real. My life in Monte Carlo was a whirlwind fairy tale. The winding roads known as "corniches," which followed the water, made for a challenging trip each time. I usually drove on the low road. Other times I used the middle road. I rarely drove on the high road, a curvy, stress-filled road that would years later be the site of the tragic car accident that took the life of Princess Grace in 1982.

David loved his time in Monte Carlo and Saint-Jean. For him it was a new adventure as well. As a young child, he was enchanted with the glamour and glitz of a magical place filled with beautiful people and numerous colorful events and festivals. The home where he boarded in Saint-Jean, Villa Rocheraie, was owned by three old-maid French sisters. They were totally devoted to David, who quickly became the master of their household. He spoke French fluently after his first few months with them. David tells me that the French Riviera experience was one of the happiest times in his life. The grand old villa, La Rocheraie, was a special place for him. The three Roche sisters most certainly have passed on. The memory of those days lives on for both of us.

Life in Monte Carlo was a constant whirlwind of Grand Prix car races, tennis opens and golf tournaments, black-tie dinners, royal galas, masked balls (a special favorite of Princess Grace), and international festivals—accompanied by an assorted parade of dukes, counts, princes, captains, and movie stars. Aristotle Onassis, Maria Callas, Estée Lauder, Rosemarie Kanzler, Robert Wagner, and Jördis and David Niven, all of whom had homes on the Riviera, were just a few of the celebrities who visited the principality as friends of the prince and princess.

Jet-setters from the Middle East, Switzerland, France, Italy, and everywhere else went in and out on the weekends. Multimillion-dollar yachts were an integral part of the social scene. I was invited once to the Onassis yacht, *Christina O*, and another time to *Xarifa*, owned by Italian businessman Carlo Traglia. The romantic goings-on between Aristotle Onassis and his mistress, Maria Callas, were a constant subject of hushed conversation and rumor.

The dapper American consul general stationed in Nice, Philip Chadbourn, was a constant guest. Once in a while, an American warship would dock in the Nice harbor. The captain would be invited to visit Monte Carlo. Captain Spence Matthews of the USS *Independence* received a big, warm welcome. The USS *John F. Kennedy* also anchored off Cannes. The Kennedy family turned out in force for the onboard reception. That ship had special significance for me. The deaths of JFK and Bobby had so greatly affected my life.

We could always count on the perennial hangers-on, the also-rans, the formers, the aging playgirls and playboys, to grace Monte Carlo with their presence. We could also count on surprise guests, such as Josephine Baker and Hugh Hefner, to drop in for a weekend.

I spent my days in an office setting. At night I was also on duty for dinners and parties. It was a decadent lifestyle filled with excess and flamboyance. I became a familiar figure around town. I was able to let my hair down from time to time, but I had to be careful and watchful, bearing in mind that I worked for Their Serene Highnesses. My actions would reflect on them.

As time went by, I began questioning my lifestyle. How many galas can a person attend in one month? How many designer gowns created by Andrew Levasseur can one own? How many stuffy dinners with Swiss bankers and playboys, conducted entirely in French, German, or Italian, can one attend? How many stagnant and stuffy all-male SBM board meetings chaired by Prince Louis de Polignac could one deal with?

Rafael Palmaro, the consul general who recruited me at Lincoln Center in New York in April 1968, visited frequently. He was pretty pleased with himself. He had brought a little bit of America to Monaco. He had held up his end of the bargain. On my end, I began to feel as if I was on a merry-go-round that never stopped. I only became grounded in reality when I left Monte Carlo to spend a few hours with David and the sisters in Saint-Jean. That for me was liberating!

I had signed up for two years of this lifestyle, and I was determined to enjoy it. But it was getting a bit tiring. Josie and I were kept very busy. She had developed a coterie of expatriate friends—rich and spoiled young people who lived in Monte Carlo year round. They adopted me from the first day. There was one party after another, usually ending up at the nightclub Les Pirates right off the high road. I'm not sure Les Pirates still exists. When I was there, it was the gathering place of the Monte Carlo elite. Looking back, it is all a big blur for me.

Josie lives in London now. She is the mother of the brilliant and beautiful English actress Sienna Miller and the up-and-coming fashion designer Savannah Miller. We reminisce frequently about the time we spent together in Monte Carlo. Josie and I remain close. I am amazed at how many details she remembers about our days and nights in Monte Carlo. Josie was my maid of honor when I married Sam in 1971. She also came to Boston for David's wedding in October 2014. She brought with her the memories of David's storied childhood years on the French Riviera.

The life of an international jetsetter is temporary and fleeting. It does not last. Some run out of money. Some run out of time. I ran out of patience and interest. I had a young child to raise. Life in Monte Carlo was exciting and spirited for a couple of years.

But after a few months in residence, I discovered that the principality was a place of intrigue and tax evasion in what some would call a mini-police-state setting. In reality the place was run by the French. General Charles de Gaulle was president of France at that time. It seemed as if there was always a crisis between Monaco and the French government. De Gaulle considered Monaco to be a French protectorate.

It was not long before I realized that all my comings and goings were being closely monitored. I never saw my watchers, but they were always there. It was almost like a European version of *Peyton Place*. Rumor mills and conspiracy theories were active and plentiful. I had unknowingly entered a world that existed in a reality all its own. There are six thousand citizens of Monaco and twenty-nine thousand tax exiles living there at any given time. Somerset Maugham, a frequent visitor to Monte Carlo, called it "a sunny place filled with shady people."

Once again, as in Geneva, Americans were viewed with suspicion and some disdain in Monaco. It was a throwback to the days of "the Ugly American." I often asked myself, "Why is it so difficult and unpleasant to be an American living and working abroad?" Ironically, many Americans

lived and some actually worked in Monaco. Grace Kelly also had difficulty being accepted by the locals when she married Prince Rainier
in 1961. After many years of hard work and dedication on her part, she
finally gained the love and admiration, not only of President de Gaulle
of France, but of the citizens of Monaco—the Monagasques.

In 1968 I had been recruited to Monte Carlo as part of Princess
Grace's strong desire to make the principality "more American." Several
years after her arrival, she decided to make an effort to attract middle-
class American tourists to the principality. And, indeed, while I was in
Monte Carlo, American-style slot machines were introduced by the
Loews Hotel chain, owned by Larry Tisch—a man whom I would meet
again in a totally different setting several years later, when we worked
together to elect Ronald Reagan as president.

The Casino de Monte-Carlo, originally funded by the French
Rothschild family, continued to allow classic European-style gaming—
baccarat, chemins de fer, and roulette. However, in order to compete
with American-style slot machines at the Loews Hotel, the casino, to
great international fanfare, grudgingly opened a "Salle des Amériques"
to attract American tourists and gambling junkets. Now, for the first time
in the history of the Casino de Monte-Carlo, you could play American
roulette, blackjack, and craps.

As an employee of the SBM, I was not allowed to enter the casino
except for social events. In retrospect that was a good thing. It shielded
me from the dark underbelly of the gambling world and the perils of
addiction and sometimes destitution that awaited many high-stake gam-
blers. My group of friends used to go to the Casino de Beaulieu a few
miles down the road in France when we had the urge to gamble. Since
almost all my expenses were covered, I made a promise to myself to save
almost all of my salary and every franc I won at the Beaulieu casino.

Many people I knew decided to visit me unexpectedly while I was
in Monaco. Friends from Geneva and New York managed to show up
regularly. I entertained them and quickly went back to work after they
left duly impressed. My sister, Sharon, visited for a few days during the

Grand Prix auto races. Coincidentally, the event was the same weekend the United States put a man on the moon. The Grand Prix was sexy and thrilling. The moonshot was earth shattering. It was a great celebration of America!

One weekend a group of us decided to go horseback riding along the Mediterranean shoreline in a breathtakingly rugged and beautiful part of southern France known as La Camargue. We were in the town of Saintes-Marie-de-la-Mer. Even though I was a fairly experienced rider, I took a fall and badly bruised my thigh on a large rock. An ambulance rushed me back to the Princess Grace Clinic in Monaco for treatment. The only surgeon on duty at the time was an abdominal surgeon. I have the scars to prove that his surgical skills were somewhat overkill for the procedure. I remained in the clinic with a massive blood clot for several days, in serious pain and feeling very embarrassed.

I never went horseback riding again, although I tend to live in areas where horses are boarded and trained. The horses bring me joy even though they remind me of that awful day in the South of France. I strongly agree with those who believe horses can be effective in thera-peutic procedures.

In 1969, during the International Television Festival in Monaco, I was invited to visit Israel by then President of Israeli Television Dr. Israel Katz. I eagerly accepted and was flown to Israel for a VIP visit. It was an extraordinary week of discovery for me. A couple of years later I would be in New York City planning US speaking tours for top-level Israeli offi-cials. As the years went by, I would visit Israel more than thirty-five times for pleasure and business. Each visit was uplifting. However, my first visit to Israel, in 1969 as an SBM executive, is the one I remember the most.

One of the highlights of the Monte Carlo social season was the Bal de la Croix-Rouge chaired by Her Serene Highness Princess Grace. Americans call it the Red Cross Ball. And plenty of Americans flew in to the principality for this sumptuous event. The high-society guests adopted me as their own private publicist for the event. Much of Palm

Beach descended on Monte Carlo, including social stalwarts like Patrick Lannan, Colonel Michael Paul, Owen Cheatham, Helen Rich, and many more. Reporters from the *Palm Beach Journal* were there to document the gowns, the romance, and the elegance of the evening presided over by Their Serene Highnesses.

The annual Red Cross Ball (Bal de la Croix-Rouge) was the highlight of the Monte Carlo social season. Hundreds of reporters and paparazzi came to town. Two years in a row I had the privilege of attending and working this spectacular international ball that generated global press coverage and funds for the International Red Cross. It was a very flamboyant event attended by international celebrities who came to see and be seen in their formal ballgowns and lavish jewels. With the sparkling French champagne flowing and the beautiful people attending it became a dream-like event for me. From year to year it never changed and the people who attended never changed. The decorations and entertainment entailed significant cost for the Grimaldi family. However, it put Monte-Carlo on the jet-set map and brought them back year after year. In effect, it was an extravagant and expensive marketing tool. The event was a chance to catch up with their friends once a year and raise money for a good cause. These type of events are held every day in many countries but none of them can match the beauty and cache of Monte-Carlo and the Palais de Casino where it was held. The guests arrived at the Palais in limousines, then photographed and announced with great titled fanfare. It was like the Oscars in Hollywood but in a more splendid and historic locale. It was a very European event – an old-style ball of yesteryear reproduced in modern times. It was an event that was unique to Monte-Carlo. For those who attended year after year it was just another gala. For me to be there in an official capacity was a memorable once in a lifetime experience.

There came a time during the two years I was in Monaco when I began to understand that the SBM leadership was seriously mired in the past. The annual events had the same format and features every year. New contemporary thinking and less traditional approaches were discouraged. So was I. It was the same old thing, year after year. They did not recruit new talent. The leadership of the SBM, influenced by their Monagasque bosses, were constrained, rigid, and locked into royal tradition. I chafed a bit at their unwillingness to try new things, to be more creative and more modern in their approach to planning events that would attract different groups of visitors to the principality. The ideas I presented would have meant change. I urged some events be geared to the younger generation. I thought it would be good to hold events in various locations around the Principality. I urged changes in the concert and ballet programming to attract a broader audience. My initiatives and ideas were not appreciated and, in some cases, frowned upon. In their view, Monte-Carlo should not change. It should remain as it was – a reminder of the privileged time of yesteryear. With the arrival of Prince Albert in the later years after I left, I assume that many things have changed.

It became abundantly clear to me that I was different from the locals. I dressed differently. I was not conspiratorial or mistrustful of others. I was perhaps too wholesome, too generous, and too friendly, as most Americans are. I often wonder if Princess Grace felt the same way. She was always so beautiful, so kind, and very understated. Princess Grace was the one, and possibly the only, American who was truly loved in the principality. The rest of us were tolerated.

I was saved by the Italians. They came to Monte Carlo in droves, and I loved them all. Sophia Loren, Maria Callas, Gianni Bulgari, Gina Lollobrigida, Virna Lisi, Carlo Traglia, and Nicola Pietrangeli stand out as notable Italian visitors who brought genuine excitement and color when they were in Monte Carlo.

When I had a chance to get out of town, I would usually go to Italy—to Milan, San Remo, Ventimiglia, Portofino, Venice, Genoa, and Santa Margherita. I also went skiing in St. Moritz, Switzerland, where I honeymooned with my first husband, Janez, and where I learned to ski. Amazingly my circumstances had changed since those days in 1959 with

Janez. This time I flew into St. Moritz on a private plane from Monte Carlo with a group of international jetsetters. I was now living in a very different world.

When I returned to my office after my brief forays out of town, I would be quietly informed by my staff about where I had been, who I had been with, and what I had done during my time away from Monte Carlo. Not a pleasant feeling for a young, single woman trying to live her life under constant monitoring. I was always amazed at how much of my personal life they knew about. Whoever they were, they were very good at watching me and quickly reporting back to the SBM authorities. I never did find out who was watching me.

In early July of 1970, as I was nearing the end of my two-year commitment, I received a phone call from home. My father was not well. He was recovering from a serious heart attack. Many questions still remained about his long-term health. It was clear the Monte Carlo fairy tale was coming to an end. It was time to go home after two years in another world—a world that would endure long after I left. I started making plans to leave, taking my memories, adventures, and love stories with me.

My second husband, Sam, and I returned to Monte Carlo thirty-five years later, in 2005. Our cruise ship pulled into the still very scenic Monte Carlo harbor. We spent the day walking around, visiting some of my favorite spots, and reminiscing about those fantasy days in the principality. My glamorous and glitzy stay in Monte Carlo had been a unique once-in-a-lifetime experience.

In 2014 Warner Brothers produced a French-American film titled *Grace of Monaco*, with the title character played by Nicole Kidman. The Grimaldis strongly objected to the way their family was depicted in the film. Director Harvey Weinstein decided to delay American distribution until 2016. The film includes a character named Phyllis Blum, an American woman who was close to Princess Grace and worked in Monte Carlo for a short time. What a coincidence…

Just recently in 2015, I learned that seven decades after the Holocaust, Monaco's Prince Albert II made the first clear public apology for the principality's role in Jewish suffering during World War II. It appears that Monaco was not the safe haven it had purported to be all these years. Albert said, "We committed the irreparable in handing over women, men and a child who had taken refuge with us. We did not protect them. It was our responsibility." He asked forgiveness for his country's role in deporting close to one hundred Jews to Nazi concentration camps and for the plundering of their assets. Monaco's chief rabbi and other Jewish figures were present when Prince Albert unveiled a monument at the Monaco cemetery carved with the names of the Jews who were deported under pressure by Nazi collaborators in France. The effort occurred as part of Prince Albert's father's desire to shed the principality's long-held reputation as a tax haven and elitist playground for the rich.

While I was living in Monte Carlo, I was unaware of its heartless wartime actions. For me, the Monaco chapter of my life had closed even further—now with dignity and compassion. Maybe one day Monte Carlo will finally join the real world.

As for me, I will always treasure the years long ago and far away that I spent in the land of the beautiful American princess, Her Serene Highness Grace Kelly.

"Those were the days my friend. I thought they'd never end." In August 1970, they did.

Starting Over Again

It was time to wake up from the Monte Carlo fantasy and get back to reality. I told Wil Groote, the director of the SBM, that I would be leaving when my contract was over in August 1970. Wil was very gracious and seemed to be genuinely sorry to see me leave. I remained in touch with him for many years after I left. On the other hand, Andre Rolfo-Fontana, the Monagasque staff member, seemed relieved that the American was leaving and taking all her new-fangled ideas back to the United States with her.

I quietly left the glittering excitement and sumptuous glamour of life in Monte Carlo, which by then had become stunningly insignificant for me. The real world was on the horizon. I wanted to do something more meaningful and substantive. I carefully laid the groundwork for life in New York City with David. I needed a place to live, a job, a housekeeper, a school for David, and money. Most of all I wanted David to have an easy transition to our next adventure in the Big Apple.

I also needed a cost-effective way back to the United States. The *Sunny Day* was docked at the Port of Cannes. Its owner, popular racy paperback author Harold Robbins, also had a private jet. He was a brilliant storyteller and one of the most popular authors of his day. He lived on the French Riviera six months a year. He had two Rolls-Royce automobiles that traveled with him between Cannes and Beverly Hills.

At about the same time I was planning to leave Monte Carlo, fifty-three-year-old Robbins was preparing to embark on a nationwide $250,000 promotion tour for his latest book, *The Inheritors*. His tenth novel was the last in a trilogy about the movie industry, preceded by *The Dream Merchants* and *The Carpetbaggers.* It was a tell-all book like the others, replete with debased language and rated very high on the vulgarity chart. His works, classified as "polite pornography," were based at least in part on his own lifestyle. Robbins's twenty previous books had sold over 750 million copies translated into dozens of languages, all published by Trident Press, a division of Simon and Schuster. Movie rights were sold concurrently with the book launch. Not surprisingly, Robbins formed a lasting friendship with Joseph E. Levine, the famed heavyweight Avco Embassy movie producer who was his neighbor on the Riviera.

I happened to see Robbins at a dinner party, and I mentioned to him that I was heading back home to New York. He offered me a flight back to the United States on his private jet. My timing was pretty good. Midway through the flight over the Atlantic Ocean, Robbins hired me as his publicist for the six-week countrywide tour to promote his latest book. It was an interesting flight. The personal interactions among those in the Robbins entourage provided a preview of things to come. At the time I didn't give it much thought. I needed a free ride home.

Robbins was accompanied on the tour by his close friend, Paul Gitlin, a flashy, overweight, cigar-smoking New Yorker who was also his agent and lawyer. Robbins was also a heavy cigarette smoker who enjoyed giant-sized cigars. His long-suffering wife, Grace, and adorable four-year-old daughter, Adrianna, were with us part of the time. Grace was an attractive brunette who seemed out of place in the flashy, fast-moving Robbins milieu. She was soft-spoken, very proper, and classy. I was not surprised to learn that in 2013 Grace Robbins wrote a tell-all book, titled "Cinderella and the Carpetbagger," about her difficult marriage to a man who suffered from "chronic infidelity." They had divorced several years before Robbins's death of respiratory heart failure in 1997.

The tour was an orgy of champagne, caviar, and young girls, and more girls, and even more girls, dropping in and out from beginning to end. Harold Robbins's life did indeed reflect the lifestyle of the characters in his sleazy novels.

In one of his many interviews, Robbins said he wrote his books "to illustrate the way we are now" and "because that's what people wanted to read about." My all-time favorite was Robbins's response that "I say and do whatever I please." Perhaps his books were bestsellers because people wanted to escape from the reality of their own lives. But for Robbins it was all about the money and the hedonistic lifestyle he wanted to continue living.

I endured personal challenges and insults from both Robbins and Gitlin, but I managed to stay on course. Because I accepted the position of publicist for the book tour, my transition from the tradition and elegance of Monte Carlo to the real world was temporarily sidetracked by the six-week exposure to the smutty, irreverent side of American pop culture represented by Harold Robbins. I completed the assignment—this time with more than a few bucks in my pocket. I was very ready for something much more uplifting…

When I finally arrived in New York in mid-September 1970, David was still visiting his father in Geneva. David had flown to Geneva as an unaccompanied minor twice a year since 1964 to spend time with his father. I was always traumatized by his departure, which began when he was three, but I knew I was doing the right thing for David.

I needed at least three months to get ready for life with David in New York. Before I left Monte Carlo, I arranged for David to attend a boarding school close to Geneva—Le Montjoie in Villars, Switzerland—for one academic quarter, until the Christmas break in mid-December. He would then fly to New York to join me. David's father would visit him regularly at the school on weekends. David, being the trusting child and sophisticated traveler that he was, accepted the arrangement without question.

I rented an apartment on New York's East Side, close to the East River, and hired a housekeeper named Mercy. The word was out that I was back in town and looking for interesting work. Within weeks of my return, I was contacted by the chief of staff of my old boss, Mayor John Lindsay. I was told the mayor had a job for me. Lucky me! They recruited me to assist with the planning for the twenty-fifth-anniversary celebration of the United Nations—an important global event for New York. The job was a one-month assignment. I rejoined the staff of the Department of Public Events, this time as an official city hostess. I was back in the limelight in New York, working with the diplomats and politicians I knew so well.

The UN's twenty-fifth birthday party was a series of events spread over several days that included receptions, dinners, concerts, and fashion shows. The guests included 14 heads of state, 127 ambassadors to the UN, and 83 consuls general, as well as New York political and business leaders. Security was intense many years before 9/11.

The theme of the city-wide celebration was embodied in the statement that "the interests that unite us are more important than the interests that divide us." The former Soviet Union, China, and Cuba made several attempts to disrupt the unity theme, but Mayor Lindsay was determined to send a message of cooperation and toleration to the world. It was not an easy task!

After the UN's birthday celebration was over I began to look for a real job. Much to my surprise, I quickly landed a position that was very meaningful and substantive. It would set my life on a completely different course.

Before tackling my next professional challenge, I decided to surprise David with a brief visit at school. I flew to Geneva and drove to the school from the airport. After meeting with the headmistress, I learned that my plans had not worked out as I hoped they would. Janez had not been able to visit David regularly. I was deeply disappointed. I asked if I could take David out of school and bring him with me to New York immediately. The headmistress told me he was doing very well and urged me to let him stay until the Christmas holiday so as not to interrupt the school quarter. With a heavy heart, I reluctantly agreed.

I joined the public-relations staff of the United Jewish Appeal (UJA) in the New York headquarters office in October 1970. They put me in charge of coordinating their roster of Israeli speakers who traveled to communities across the United States to help raise funds and support for the State of Israel.

My position enabled me to travel and spend quality time with Ambassador Abba Eban, Prime Minister Golda Meir, General Moshe Dayan, Prime Minister Yitzhak Rabin, and many other Israeli luminaries of the day. I also traveled to Israel, Poland, Romania, and the Netherlands to attend overseas UJA conferences. I was back in the groove again!

It was another dream job! I had finally landed in a spot where I could do something significant and rewarding. My parents had imbued me with a strong sense of Zionism and a deep attachment to the Jewish people and the State of Israel. After life as a jetsetter, I was finally able to do my part and make my parents proud. Working on Israel's behalf gave my life meaning and purpose.

It was a breezy fall day in early November 1970. On my first UJA assignment, I walked into a meeting room at the Holiday Inn in Irwin, Pennsylvania, just outside of Pittsburgh. Members of the Young Leadership Division of the Tri-State Area (eastern Ohio, southwestern Pennsylvania, and west Virginia) of the UJA were discussing plans for an upcoming regional conference. I noticed a handsome young man sitting at the head table. I could feel that my life was about to change once again. To this day I'm not sure exactly what happened at that meeting. It must have been love at first sight for both of us. His name was Sam Kaminsky, a young attorney from Johnstown, Pennsylvania.

I knew I wanted to see Sam again. I took the initiative and called to make sure he was planning to attend the Annual UJA Conference at the New York Hilton in early December. He assured me he would be there. Thus began a whirlwind courtship that started with our first date at Orsini's restaurant, followed by many evenings at Le Club and Studio 54.

As planned, David arrived in New York a week before Christmas on a snowy, blustery night. His plane, scheduled to land at Kennedy Airport, was diverted to Baltimore because of the bad weather. Finally, the plane landed, and David arrived at two o'clock in the morning. The stewardess brought him to me. He was wearing the navy-blue V-neck sweater I had knit for him that matched his amazing big, blue eyes. I dissolved in tears at the sight of him. I was overjoyed to have him home with me to start our new life together in New York, once again.

The story ended happily a few months later on June 24, 1971, when I married Sam in a small and elegant wedding at the Trianon Room of the Carlyle Hotel, accompanied by an evening of famed Bobby Short playing the piano at the renowned Carlyle Café.

Steeltown Usa

I visited Johnstown, Pennsylvania, for the first time during Christmas week in 1970. Sam and I attended a holiday party hosted by Jeanne and Rob Gleason. That evening would be my introduction to the Johnstown elite. I arrived at the party wearing black velvet hot pants and high boots, which were the current fashion rage in New York. The reaction on the faces of the guests, especially the women, at the party told me all I needed to know. I had made a major faux pas. Johnstown had not yet caught up with New York fashion trends. I pulled it off but was very embarrassed. Sam didn't seem to mind. I realized then and there that I was entering another world far different from the fast-paced life I was leaving behind. Jeanne Gleason is one of my closest friends and an accomplished woman in her own right. Whenever we are together, the "hot-pants incident" comes up, and we all have a good laugh.

After the June wedding Sam and I left New York and drove to Johnstown to start our new life together. Sam had told me many times that Johnstown was a little like Switzerland. When I arrived in town, I realized very quickly that he had exaggerated a bit. Yes, there was the beautiful scenery of the foothills of the Allegheny Mountains. But there were the steel mills and the coal mines as well. There also was the man I loved.

Being a big-city girl, I had never lived in a house. We had always lived in apartments in large buildings. When we pulled into the garage of our new home in Johnstown, the anticipation and excitement overwhelmed me. I jumped out of the car while Sam was unloading our bags from the trunk. I accidentally pushed the button that makes the garage door come down and almost killed Sam. He quickly dove out of the way. He looked at me afterward and jokingly asked, "Did you marry me for the life insurance"? It was clear then I had a lot to learn about life in small-town America.

Sam was born in Johnstown. Instead of striking out in the big city after law school, he chose to return to his hometown and be there for his widowed mother. As the oldest of three children, he felt it his responsibility. His father, Louis, had died when Sam was thirteen. Overnight he had become the man of the family. His grandparents, who were rabbis, came to Johnstown from eastern Europe in the 1880s. It was the place where the Kaminsky family had started their new lives in America.

Some Jewish immigrants in the area worked in the mills and mines, while others created an economy that centered on trades and mercantile shops within their ethnic neighborhoods. At one time there were three synagogues in Johnstown. As the community began to prosper, they moved from the downtown Johnstown area to the suburb of Westmont. The three synagogues have now merged into one. When I came to Johnstown, there were about 1,500 Jews left from a peak of 2,000 in the 1950s. Many had already left to seek educational and business opportunities elsewhere. The synagogue congregations have become smaller and smaller.

I quickly discovered that, in addition to Sam's involvement with the Young Leadership Division of the UJA and his dedication to Jewish causes and the State of Israel, he was an institution in Johnstown. He knew everyone in town, and everyone knew and respected him. As he used to tell me, he was "a big fish in a small pond." He was a popular general-practice attorney specializing in family law, and he was very good at it. I could never be sure whether Sam had handled divorce, custody, or estate issues of the people we knew socially. All I know is that there have been an awful lot of women who swore by him and sent him gifts at holiday time over the years.

Phyllis Kaminsky

With Sam came his four children, Sherry, Louis, Jay, and Phillip, from his first marriage, to Barbara Handmaker of Altoona, Pennsylvania. Being a stepmother was the biggest challenge that awaited me in my new life, and it was an outsized challenge. Sam's oldest son, Louis, came to live with us. The other children stayed with their mother, who eventually left Johnstown and moved to Tucson, Arizona. I spent many years trying to reconcile with Sam's children, who were not pleased with their father's new bride. Barbara passed away of cancer in 1986.

I am now proud to be their mom and a grandma to their eight children. Each one of the children and grandchildren is special in his or her own way. Our lives together would not have been easy had we not found a way to love and respect one another. After all these years, I am confident I have earned their trust and friendship. The road was not easy, but it was one worth traveling.

One winter in the late seventies, we decided to take the whole family skiing in Sun Valley. We had a great vacation—no broken legs—and after a week of sun, powder snow, and bonding, we flew back to Boise, Idaho, on two small chartered airplanes. Sam's children were in one plane, which left a couple of minutes before the second plane that held Sam, myself, David, and Glenn. The first plane landed in Boise without incident. The second plane ran into a dangerous ice storm. The wings iced up instantly. I was shrieking with fear. Sam turned white, David put on his earphones to listen to music, and Glenn threw up. Luckily, our brilliant, red-cheeked, sweating pilot managed to land us in Boise at the far end of the runway. We threw ourselves onto the icy ground and began hugging each other and crying tears of relief. Ten or more years later, Louis, Sam's oldest son, would become a very successful private aircraft broker. The family never again flew together on a private plane. We had come way too close to try that again.

I settled down to a more relaxed life as the wife of a successful small-town lawyer. And for a number of years, life was good. I was content. Sam and I added Glenn to the mix of five children from our previous marriages. His birth in March 1974 gave me new life, lifted my spirits, and drew Sam and me closer to one another. We were loved and well taken care of. I became involved in community activities. I filled my days with Johnstown Symphony Committee meetings and various charity events. I also remained active with Israel-related organizations and continued to do special projects for the UJA. From time to time, I visited local organizations and schools and gave speeches about Israel and the Middle East region.

On one of my overseas trips, I met a Canadian woman named Elaine Dubow. We hit it off and became good friends. We were both strong supporters of Israel and very motivated to get involved and do something. We would become partners in a pioneering effort to complement the recently signed Camp David Accords. We thought about it for a couple of years and gave birth to our concept in 1979—the Jerusalem Women's Seminar. It would be an extraordinary adventure that affected the lives of many women. More about that later…

To keep busy, I took a correspondence course at the New York School of Interior Design. I earned a certification as an interior designer. I started a company called Interior Innovations, with clients in Johnstown and Pittsburgh. My specialty was color coordination. I also worked part-time at a local furniture store and picked up several clients. I never intended it to be a lifetime career; however, my design expertise has stayed with me and been put to good use for family and friends.

One of the highlights of my time in Johnstown was working with city leaders in a national competition for recognition as the All-American City. Johnstown won in 1972. The award gave a big boost to a town that was having difficulty adjusting to the negative economic changes affecting the steel and coal industrial base. Johnstown was chosen because it represented the best of America: a diverse immigrant population struggling to maintain a good quality of life for its citizens who were religious, hardworking, honest, and patriotic.

Five years later the Johnstown flood in July of 1977 devastated the area. It rained all night. We slept through the downpour of 11 inches of rain that had drenched the area in a few hours. We awoke the next morning to learn that the downtown area was destroyed. Part of Sam's office building floated down the Stonycreek River. The drinking water turned brown. Debris was everywhere. Desolation was widespread. Houses and people had been swept away by the force of the water. Our home was not affected because we were located on the high ground overlooking the city. Johnstown and its surrounding suburbs faced an even greater economic disaster. Over the years, the city has slowly been rebuilt and refurbished. But the All-American City never completely recovered from one of the greatest natural disasters in the history of America.

The aftermath of the disastrous flood in 1977 was awful. Sam insisted that Glenn and I fly to New York to stay with my folks in White Plains until things got better. I could not know at the time that those would be the last weeks of my father's life. So as a result of the Johnstown flood, I was fortunate to be able to spend a few days with my father before he passed away suddenly on July 31, 1977.

When Sam and I think of our lives in Johnstown, we remember Mrs. Mathilda Smith. She will always have a special place in our heart. From the moment Glenn started talking she became "Mazar" She was our housekeeper for over twenty years in Johnstown and then followed us to Maryland for many more years. Mazar never gave up working until she was in her late 80s. She was the best example of Johnstown. She was honest, devoted to our family and hard working.

We also share family memories of playing the game Jeopardy. Even though there was a thirteen-year age difference between Glenn and David, they were very competitive with each other. The two children were trying to outdo each other. It made for many funny moments when we were living together in Johnstown. David had his own room and bathroom at one end of the house. He would be often found playing with building blocks and electric trains in the basement playroom. Glenn was busy learning to walk and talk at the other end of the house. The other children welcomed Glenn into the family. He would always be the "baby" who was universally loved by all. Sam and I now had six children. Our family get-togethers were lively events.

Our family pet was Spritzer, a pure-bred gray and white schnauzer whose original name was Baron von Spritzer VII. We brought him into our family early to help David adjust to Johnstown. When David left for college at Princeton in 1979, Spritzer died within a week. I always believed Spritzer died of a broken heart. James Thurber has written, "In his grief over the loss of a dog, a little boy stands for the first time on tiptoe, peering into the rueful morrow of manhood." And so it was for David.

The years in Johnstown were good years. My parents visited frequently driving down from the New York City area. I made wonderful lifelong friends, and Sam and I traveled frequently

I was a registered Republican when I married Sam in 1971. He was a long-time activist in Pennsylvania Democratic Party politics. He urged me to register as a Democrat. I did so reluctantly. However, the policies of the Carter administration troubled me greatly. So in 1979 I changed my registration again and became a Republican. I also decided to get involved in national politics. I let my Republican friends know that I was interested in joining the presidential campaign of 1980.

Sam sensed my restlessness. He gave me unlimited love and support. Sam is a wise man.

The Jerusalem Women's Seminar

It was March 26, 1979. Sam and I were at the White House dinner to celebrate the signing of the Camp David Accords. Our dinner companions were former Senator and Mrs. Alan Cranston of California and Dina and Gamal Sadat, the son and daughter of President Anwar Sadat. We were truly honored to be seated with members of the Sadat family. By the end of the dinner, we were good friends. The Sadats invited us to visit Egypt as their personal guests. In 1979 the air was filled with euphoria, optimism, and a large dose of history. I remember it as a windy spring night on the White House lawn. It was a "stupendous achievement" according to Ambassador-at-Large Arthur Goldberg. When Israeli Prime Minister Menachem Begin and Egyptian President Anwar Sadat walked off the stage arm in arm, the audience was jubilant and cautiously hopeful for the future. The guests felt they were part of a truly momentous event. They were treated to entertainment by an Egyptian trio and Israeli violinists Pinchas Zukerman and Itzhak Perlman, topped by Leontyne Price, the famed American soprano. It was the largest White House state dinner in recent memory, with 1,300 guests, including President and Mrs. Carter, mingling and table-hopping like at a Jewish bar mitzvah party.

"In ancient days God promised Abraham that from his seed would come many nations, and that promise has been fulfilled," said President Carter in his moving toast. "Yet for much too long, the people of Israel and the people of Egypt—two of the nations of the Children of Abraham trusting in the same God, hoping for the same peace…knew only enmity between them…That time, thank God, is at an end," said Carter.

I decided to take the Sadat family up on their invitation to visit Egypt and asked my Canadian friend, Elaine Dubow, to accompany me. We had been talking for several years about what we could do as women to further the goals of peace in the Middle East. The signing of the Camp David Accords gave us the courage and incentive to move forward to play our part in bringing people together in the Middle East. We decided to strike while the iron was hot.

In the summer of 1979, the adventure for Elaine and me began in Athens when we boarded Olympic Airlines Flight 325 bound for Cairo, Egypt. There were no direct flights from Israel to Egypt. Once we boarded our flight in Athens, we were in uncharted territory. Having visited Israel a few days earlier, and to make the point of who we were, we carried our Israeli shopping bags and that day's *Jerusalem Post*. We were on our way.

The plane was filled with assorted Arabs and a smattering of European and Asian businessmen. Everyone looked at us, but no one spoke to us. Upon our arrival at the Cairo airport, the hundred or so people on our flight combined with the thousands in the airport terminal to become a sea of humanity. This same sea of humanity was to be a constant part of our lives for the next four days.

The taxi ride to the Nile Hilton Hotel in the center of Cairo, supposedly only fifteen miles from the airport, took one and a half hours through the most harrowing traffic and the worst driving I have ever experienced. We discovered that there are no speed limits in Egypt and few operational traffic lights. It was a chaotic and frightening experience.

It was during this nerve-racking drive to the hotel that we got our first glimpse of the well-known Cairo bus scenes: hundreds of people scrambling for one bus and then hanging on for dear life with arms and legs dangling out of windows. We also saw people sleeping and eating on the sidewalks; many unfinished buildings; and construction workers' tent camps next to dilapidated office buildings. All of this was in contrast to the many beautiful statues at major intersections and the opulent Middle Eastern nightclubs with names like Safari and Phoenix, adjacent to the delicate, ornate architecture of the numerous Islamic mosques.

By the time we arrived at our hotel, we felt dirty and very thirsty. Cairo is hot and it is gritty. There is dust in the air, and if there is a slight breeze from the desert, it brings the sand with it. We were tired, hungry, and emotionally drained. In 1979 Americans were very popular in Egypt. Jimmy Carter was a national hero, and Egyptians were naming their children after him. We heard "you are welcome"—a common refrain from hotel staff—no less than fifteen times before we finally got to our hotel room. From the outset, we found the Egyptians to be extremely polite, warm, charming, hospitable, and gentle.

When we made it to our room, we immediately ran to the window to see the Nile River. And there it was on the right. The river that makes the country. We had heard many times that "Egypt is the Nile and the Nile is Egypt."

To our left were the central train station and, again, the hordes of people moving almost aimlessly through the city streets to the sound of the constantly honking car horns.

I was amazed at the gentility of the people in contrast to the harshness of their daily lives. Egyptian men were in Western-style leisure suits and carrying attaché cases, while others wore colorful galabias or caftans, contrasting with Egyptian women in jeans and T-shirts and those wearing the traditional chador, their heads wrapped in black and their faces veiled. I was able to distinguish the Copts in their priestly robes and their women in the customary white headdress from the Yemeni blacks and the tall, agile Nubians from the Sudan, all blending together in an unforgettable kaleidoscope of a Cairo street scene.

Life in Cairo begins when the traffic dies down a bit. We had dinner every night at ten or later. One night we dined in the shadow of the Pyramids, another night with European tourists on the Nile, and a third night with well-to-do Egyptians in the Cairo suburb of Heliopolis. Every night we saw belly dancers at dinner.

After two sleepless nights at the Nile Hilton, we decided to move to the El-Salam Hotel in Heliopolis to escape the noise and congestion. I was beginning to worry about whether or not we would get to the Cairo airport in time to make our flight back to Athens and Israel. Heliopolis was close to the airport, so our chances improved slightly.

Egyptians expressed a deep dislike of their rich Arab brethren, especially Saudi Arabians and Libyans. Our taxi drivers described their Arab brothers thus: "They come from the desert on their camels with much money and nothing more. They do not help the poor but come to Egypt only to show they are rich." At the Nile Hilton gambling casino, where a few months before one could have seen the princes of Saudi Arabia and the sheikhs and emirs from the Gulf, there were now empty seats. The Arab boycott of Egypt was in effect. Punishment for signing a peace treaty with Israel. Egyptians told us they expected that the seats would soon fill up with Germans, Japanese, Americans, and Scandinavians, and they seemed pleased that the "rich animals" were staying away.

The Egyptians are very proud people. They believe that they were able to make peace with Israel because they were strong, had a fast-growing population of more than forty-one million, and won the October 1973 War. Egyptians believed that the peace treaty would transform their country from a poor wasteland into an economic oasis. Once a relatively well-endowed economy, Egypt had suffered runaway inflation and lack of industrial growth due to the past three decades of war. Sadat was planning new agricultural-development projects and a system of fresh-water canals to make Egypt self-sufficient in eggs, chicken, and dairy products in three years. The project was never completed. President Anwar Sadat was assassinated on October 6, 1981. Many of Sadat's dreams for his people went unfulfilled. It is generally assumed that he was killed by the Muslim Brotherhood, but it has never been proven. The Muslim Brotherhood, a powerful political force in Egypt, opposed the Camp David Accords.

Egyptians pride themselves on having the largest number of college graduates in the Arab world. They supplied teachers to many Arab countries until the recent boycott. While we were in Egypt, the imam of Gaza, a Palestinian who had accepted the elements of the Camp David Accords, was assassinated by the PLO. But the Egyptians assured us that "there will be others to take his place." I felt comforted that a process of peaceful accommodation between Israel and Egypt had truly begun.

Separating each major city in Egypt is the ever-present desert—miles and miles of uncultivated, unpopulated, barren sand. That desert is very different from the Sinai, with its starkly dramatic rock formations and magnificent beaches that Elaine and I knew so well. We visited the city of Ismailia on the Suez Canal. We sailed down the Suez Canal in a patrol boat. The pontoon bridges the Egyptians had used to cross the canal in the War of 1973 were still there. The shorelines are so close that people can carry on a clear conversation while standing on opposite sides of the Canal. Our captain told us that they talked to the Israelis that way almost daily. We heard the sounds of an Israel pop-music radio station playing on his radio as we motored through the canal in the direction of Port Said. The Egyptians are very proud of the Suez Canal. The passage fees from the seventy-five to one hundred ships that pass through the canal provide an economic lifeline for the country.

We were taken aboard the presidential yacht for the royal tour and a reception in our honor as guests of President and Mrs. Sadat. The guests were unanimous in their desire for "no more war" and "no more Russians." They truly believed that now Israel and Egypt would work together, with America as their partner. They all wanted to visit Israel. They believed that Israel was in the same state of poverty and economic chaos as Egypt. Elaine and I knew otherwise, but we said nothing as we nodded in agreement.

Many times we heard the word "shalom" shouted at us by store merchants, taxi drivers, and people in the street. And, of course, we visited the Pyramids and the Sphinx. We saw the sound and light show that illustrated one hundred thousand Egyptian workers united in a surge of faith—an army of laborers with a mystical force dedicated to their kings and the pharaohs. The deputy prime minister of Israel, Yigael Yadin, was visiting at the same time, and Egyptian security was everywhere. A new era had dawned. Egyptian police were guarding an Israeli dignitary who had come to study the archaeological treasures of this ancient civilization.

I now understand why some Egyptians say, "We are not Arabs. We are pharaohs. We are different from the other Arabs who come to Cairo."

My trip to Egypt presented many challenges and contrasts. From one of my hotel rooms, I could see the abject poverty of a mud hut across the unpaved road. The scene disturbed me. I experienced the maddening frustration of not being able to make any phone calls during the four days I was in Egypt because the telephone system simply did not work. I heard American music and colloquialisms everywhere we went. And we did indeed miss our flight from Cairo to Athens on our way back to Israel. I also remember some very special moments when Egyptians referred to Israelis as their cousins, and our driver, Badir, bid us "shalom" as he dropped us off for the last time, while clutching in his hand the Israeli one-hundred-pound note we had given him to spend when he visited Israel.

During our final farewell with President and Mrs. Sadat, they reminded us that Egyptians are very emotional people. They can love as intensely as they can hate. President Sadat had ordered plastic white doves of peace to be hung from street lamps and in flower pots at the president's residence in Giza, and banners proclaiming peace hung on all the main city squares. The Egyptian people were surrounded by constant reminders that their country had taken a dramatic and different turn in history—a turn away from war. Anwar Sadat knew and understood his people well. He was a man of the people, of the Egyptian masses, and he believed that his people wanted a better life. He went to Jerusalem and changed history. He knew that if he did not show courage and determination, his beloved country and its proud people would lose the ultimate battle—the struggle to survive.

The road ahead, we were told by an Egyptian journalist, is covered with rough-edged heavy stones, "the kind that were used to build the pyramids." We told them that we wanted to believe that the Egyptian soldiers we saw on our visit would soon be working on the building of bridges and cities of peace even if the bridges and cities were named after battles of the October 1973 War. We briefly talked to Jehan Sadat about what women could do to help nurture the historic peace treaty. She said that she was also thinking along the same lines. We should stay in touch, she said. Elaine and I took her at her word that day in Cairo. Jehan Sadat never disappointed.

Before we left Elaine and I learned about the Cairo car-rental agency that was a front operation for the PLO run by Mohammed Arafat, brother of Yāsser Arafat. We also learned about the City of the Dead, where the poorest of Egyptians use the headstones and mausoleums of an old Cairo cemetery as their homes. We experienced a short shaky camel trip in front of the Pyramids; the magnificent exhibits of the Islamic Museum; the massive traffic jams and lack of paved roads or alternate routes to anywhere; the Khan el-Khalili, as the Cairo marketplace is called; and the smells and sounds of ancient Araby. And last but not least, we laughed about the treasured bottles of mineral water that we carried with us everywhere to protect our delicate Western tummies from the ravages of Pharaoh's plague.

I will never forget returning to Israel from Athens and driving into Jerusalem with an Egyptian-Jewish cab driver quite by coincidence. Once again I rushed to the window of a hotel room and saw the golden lights of the magic place where it began for all of us.

The people of Israel and Egypt are different. Israelis are independent, ambitious, highly spirited, and sometimes abrasive. Egyptians are gentle, plodding, and inefficient, yet almost always charming. The key to peace rests with them. Their soldiers should meet in bars rather than on battlefields; their children should study together; their businessmen should make deals; and their lives should become intertwined.

In four short days, we learned that human contact and dialogue are the essence of peace. And thus was born the idea that we had been thinking about since we first met at a women's conference in Amsterdam. Elaine and I cofounded the Jerusalem Women's Seminar (JWS).

The JWS, as we called it, was born in early 1980. It involved prominent professional North American women in an intensive interfaith dialogue with women representing the diverse cultures and ethnic groups of the Middle East. Central to the JWS experience was a highly organized study tour in Israel and Egypt. The program matched women, including Israelis, Palestinians, and Egyptians, with their career counterparts representing the three major religious denominations that have historic ties to the city of Jerusalem. A ten-day peer-to-peer exchange focused on the core idea that human contact and dialogue could bring about peaceful and tolerant relationships. Through the JWS, women of North America and the Middle East had an opportunity to reach out to one another in an atmosphere of mutual learning, understanding, and respect.

Elaine and I drew on the strength of our own personal beliefs, and were inspired by Loren Eiseley's characterization of women as "the eternally civilizing influence of mankind." We believed that women's voices of reason and understanding were needed to support the idea of a permanent peace in the Middle East.

Our Sponsors Committee consisted of Author Phyllis Chesler, Actress Colleen Dewhurst, the Honorable Millicent Fenwick, the Honorable Clare Boothe Luce, the Honorable Bess Myerson, the Honorable Pat Schroeder, Sister Ann Patrick Ware, and several others. Yona Goldberg was our very competent and dedicated executive director.

In 1980 the first group of JWS participants called themselves "Sisters of the Bus." The JWS lived and made news and friends for four years. In all, sixty-seven women from the United States and Canada participated and shared thoughts and ideas with countless Israeli, Egyptian, and Palestinian women. Among them were Dr. Frances Hesselbein, Ambassador Helene von Damm, Pia Lindström, Sister Colette Mahoney, Reverend Elizabeth Scott, Judge (ret.) Patricia Wald, Governor Liz Carpenter, Betsey Wright, Ursula Meese, Nancy Reynolds, Dr. Rosemary Ruether, Wilma Espinoza, Charlayne Hunter-Gault, Sister Jane Scully, Kate Rand Lloyd, Gail Sheehy, Carolyn Deaver, Carol McCain, the Honorable Iona Campagnolo and, Senator Yvette Rousseau from Canada, and many more.

JWS participants were inspired by the inimitable Ruth Dayan, who, now in her nineties, still continues her handicrafts work with Palestinian women through the company she created, known as Maskit.

Raymonda Tawil and her daughter, Suha, came to Jerusalem from the West Bank to meet the JWS women several times. An openness and spirit of cooperation lasted for just a short time. Suha went on to marry Y sir Arafat, and the rest is history.

Until that dark day in October 1981 when Anwar Sadat was assassinated, Jehan Sadat and more than twenty-five prominent Egyptian women and more than a hundred Israeli women shared the JWS dream with us. Jehan welcomed the Israeli participants with open arms. In August 1981 she talked about future joint projects and the advancement of women in the Middle East. A few months later, Anwar Sadat was gone. The program struggled on after Hosni Mubarak became president of Egypt. Suzy Mubarak tried to keep it going, but Jehan Sadat was irreplaceable as the inspirational keystone in Egypt.

In October 1982, President Reagan presented the American Friendship Medal to President Anwar el-Sadat posthumously at a White House ceremony in recognition of his "personal courage and perseverance in the cause of peace; for his bold leadership and talent in achieving a peace no one dared to imagine; and for his example to all who would serve the cause of peace and freedom." Jehan Sadat accepted the medal on her late husband's behalf. There was not a dry eye in the house.

In 1983 the JWS sadly retired as a fond memory and valiant effort by all involved. The long march of history had overtaken our mission. Some of our colleagues suggested Elaine and I should be nominated for a Nobel Peace Prize for our contribution to the normalization process of the Camp David Accords. Elaine and I laughed it off. In our hearts, when Anwar Sadat was struck down by an alleged Muslim Brotherhood bullet, Elaine and I knew our dream had died with him. The momentum for cooperation had been lost. In 1976 two Irish women, Betty Williams and Mairead Corrigan, had indeed been recognized for their work to bring about reconciliation in Ireland. For the JWS, it was not to be.

Nevertheless, something very important and meaningful did happen to many women from the United States, Canada, Israel, and Egypt for four years during the late seventies and early eighties. In its time JWS was a call to act, to be involved, to reach out, and to share. The JWS touched the lives of hundreds of women who are out there somewhere still dreaming and remembering that brief life-changing moment in time that was the Jerusalem Women's Seminar.

The Political Bug

In 1979 Sam gave me my wings and let me fly. He encouraged me to get back in the game. So I did. I called Gordon Zacks, a top leader in the Jewish community and a Republican Party activist. Gordy was my mentor and supporter when I worked at the UJA before I married Sam. He was a close personal friend of George H. W. Bush. I told him I was interested in joining the Bush campaign. Shortly thereafter, Pete Teeley, press secretary of the campaign, called and recruited me as a press specialist for the Pennsylvania and Illinois primaries. In the meantime, our friend Rob Gleason from Johnstown had become a major player in the Republican Party of Pennsylvania. I now had some excellent contacts and was part of the primary season activity in 1979.

My marriage was strong enough to withstand the pressures and conflict of American politics. Over the years Sam gradually mellowed into an independent voter from a lifelong Democrat, which, in my view, can be considered progress.

The Bush 41 campaign was unsuccessful, and I was sure my short political career was over. Ronald Reagan won the nomination in August 1980 at the Detroit convention. At the time of the convention, I was in Israel with the first group of women chosen to be part of the Jerusalem Women's Seminar. To my surprise I received a phone call—this time from Max Fisher, the dean of Jewish Republicans and a political icon in Detroit. He had a job for me. He asked me to join the Reagan-Bush campaign as deputy director of voter outreach, working with Larry Goldberg, Max Hugel, and Elizabeth Dole. I'm quite sure my good friend Gordon

Zacks primed the pump for me behind the scenes. It was because of him that I received the opportunity of a lifetime—to join the Reagan-Bush team. I jumped at the chance to make history as part of the Reagan for President campaign. I embarked on another great adventure that would determine the path of my life and career for more than thirty years.

I traveled the country with Ed Meese, Jim Baker, Mike Deaver, Elizabeth Dole, and many other high-level campaign officials. Our goal was to accomplish what had never been done before by the Republican Party: gain a significant percentage of the Jewish vote. We traversed the country for three months, meeting with community leadership in many different States. Whenever I spoke to a Jewish women's group, inevitably I would get the question, "How can a smart Jewish woman like you be a Republican?" My answer was short and to the point. "Jewish voters have to be active in both political parties. Otherwise, our votes will be taken for granted." That response seemed to satisfy, because there were no more questions on that topic.

The Jewish outreach effort was very successful. The Reagan-Bush ticket garnered 39 to 40 percent of the Jewish vote. Those votes, added to those cast by "Reagan Democrats," made a huge difference in the final outcome and greatly contributed to our 1980 landslide victory. I had passed through my political baptism by fire. The future looked bright. It was a Reagan-Bush ticket!

I went on to join the Reagan Transition Team based in Alexandria, Virginia. If you are part of the transition, you can be fairly certain of being appointed to a position in the incoming administration. For three months I worked long hours, attended interminable meetings, and laid the groundwork for my future career. Sam, of course, was always supportive and enthusiastic about my future.

He agreed to what is now known in social parlance as a "commuter marriage." Our six-year-old son, Glenn, joined me in the DC area. Sam stayed behind in Johnstown. David had started college at Princeton. Sam was my charming escort, faithfully driving three and a half hours from Johnstown almost every weekend to be with us. We tried to talk on the phone every day to keep up with all the gossip and happenings at both ends. Coming together on weekends was always special. Our marriage was strong, and the commuter arrangement, while not ideal, allowed us to enjoy our personal freedom and space. Thus began a long commute that lasted for twenty-three years.

Commuter marriages were rather common among Reagan appointees, many of whom had spouses who lived in California or the western United States. Women, especially, took up the challenge to serve in the Reagan administration. The concept of a commuter-marriage lifestyle was widely covered at the time by the news media. Sam was quoted in one of the articles as saying, "It has taken time to adjust to living in different places during the week, but I feel that because my wife has a job she enjoys, the marriage has been strengthened. Phyllis is happier and the marriage is better for it." Women were on the move, inspired by the desire to pursue high-powered careers previously unavailable to them. I was one of them.

On January 21, 1981, I followed my campaign colleagues into the White House. I was now an official foot soldier in the Reagan Revolution as press officer on the National Security Council. They were heady days for all of us.

THAT WAS THE CAMPAIGN;
THIS IS THE WHITE HOUSE

It was January 21, 1981. A new beginning for America. The Inaugural Balls were over. The Reagan Revolution had begun. Our country had a "rendezvous with destiny." The Reaganauts were ready to roll. I was one of them.

I had a lot to learn, and it would happen fast. I was escorted to my new office in the Old Executive Office Building (OEOB), an old, cavernous building with endless hallways and few restrooms. My office was very large. The furnishings were government ugly. I was now the official press officer for the National Security Council (NSC), headed by Richard V. Allen, the newly appointed national-security advisor.

I sat down to take it all in and noticed a paper on my desk titled "Talking Points for Sale of AWACS to Saudi Arabia." This must be a joke, I thought to myself. I had spent the last six months telling Jewish groups around the country that President Reagan would not sell AWACS to Saudi Arabia. Every major pro-Israel organization strongly opposed the sale. I looked again. The paper appeared to be official White House/NSC letterhead. I jumped off my chair and found my way out of the OEOB maze of offices. I crossed over to the West Wing of the White House, where the newly appointed senior staff members were also just arriving at their new workplace. I breached protocol and strode into Dick Allen's office waving the piece of paper. I asked him whether or not the talking-points message could be a mistake or a bad joke.

"I've spent the last six months of my life denying it would happen, and my credibility would be shot," I said excitedly.

Dick Allen looked slightly amused as he prepared to give me my first important lesson in politics. He said, "Phyllis, that was the campaign; this is the White House."

I was shocked and confused, but I heard the message loud and clear. As I slowly and sheepishly backed out of his office, I remember saying something to the effect of "I recuse myself from being involved in this, Dick."

To his credit Dick Allen did, in fact, keep me away from the matter. The AWACS sale was a hot potato for the new administration. The Departments of State and Defense did not want to deal with it. It was left to Dick Allen to carry out the president's directive. Saudi Arabia did eventually receive their AWACS. Colonel Ollie North became a nation-wide celebrity as a result of his involvement. For me the entire AWACS issue left an indelible mark on my career in politics. Politics was a tough and dirty business. I moved on suitably chastened and a lot wiser.

During the campaign, I became friendly with several women who were very close to the president: Nancy Reynolds, a long-time friend of the Reagans; Ursula Meese, the wife of the White House counselor; and Helene von Damm, personal secretary to the president. These three wonderful women adopted me and took me under their wing. Little did I know at the time how important these women would become during my time at the White House and long afterward. Ursula, Nancy and Helene became participants in the JWS in the summer of 1981. It was my way of thanking them for welcoming me into their world.

Life as a White House staffer was a whirlwind. State dinners, official ceremonies, historic events, glamorous parties, high-level meetings, embassy receptions, and the daily White House press briefings became my life. My friends made sure that I missed very few events. I was treated as an insider—an A-lister.

Sam the Democrat would find himself seated next to the chairman of Occidental Petroleum at a Republican Eagles dinner or next to a foreign diplomat at a State Department function and wonder how to introduce himself. He took it all in stride and introduced himself as "Phyllis's husband."

In late 1981 the president appointed Sam to be a member of a Department of Energy bipartisan advisory commission on alternative fuels facilities. Because he was born and raised in southwest Pennsylvania, his knowledge of the coal-mining aspect of the energy sector enabled him to play a meaningful role on the commission for several years.

The White House is a very special place. While working there, you are well aware that you are part of history. The honor of being selected to serve President Reagan was beyond exciting. It was exhilarating! The president lit up every room he entered with his broad smile and sunny personality. He always had a kind word or a wave and handshake to greet you. He was a deeply principled conservative leader with a populist streak. He called himself a "citizen politician." He was also so much smarter than he was portrayed to be by the mainstream media. He was humbled by the honor given to him when the people asked him to lead them. He had faith in the goodness of people. He loved the American people even though some of them did not love him. He never stopped listening to them. He apologized when a policy went awry. He adjusted his thinking to what he perceived to be the wishes of the majority of Americans, most of whom were very cynical about their leaders and government when he became president. Ronald Reagan unified the country as never before. He made us proud to be Americans. I look back on those eight years as the best years of my life. I was thrilled and honored to be a small part of it.

President Reagan's inaugural address in 1981 has had a soothing and lasting impact on my thinking until this day, specifically the part about the privilege of being American. He said, "The...ills we suffer have come upon us over several decades. They will not go away in days, weeks, or months, but they will go away. They will go away because we, as Americans, have the capacity now, as we have had in the past, to do whatever needs to be done to preserve this last and greatest bastion of freedom." He also said, "As for the enemies of freedom, those who are potential adversaries, they will be reminded that peace is the highest aspiration of the American people. We will negotiate for it, sacrifice for it; we will not surrender for it—now or ever." These words have stayed with me all these years. They are uppermost in my mind at a time when America faces a new set of problems and challenges around the world.

David was at Princeton studying architecture during the Reagan years. He became a champion debater. He went on to a graduate degree in architecture from Harvard. After graduation he chose to remain in Boston, where he launched his very successful architectural career.

Glenn was with me in Maryland. He was a happy, busy child with lots of friends. He did well at school. I tried very hard to keep up with his soccer games and tennis matches on the weekends. It was a constant challenge.

On March 30, 1981, the day of the assassination attempt on President Reagan, the White House was in turmoil. Somehow, in the midst of the chaos, I found myself sitting on a sofa in the Situation Room near Dick Allen's basement office. Senior administration officials were gathering there to assess the situation. Dick Allen entered, saw me sitting there, and told me to leave. I don't remember how I got there in the first place. There was so much going on in the White House. Staffers were not sure what they were supposed to do. I jumped up from the sofa and made my way to my regular seat in the front row of the press briefing room in another part of the White House. When General Al Haig, the secretary of state, strode in, grabbed the microphone, stood behind the podium, and said, "I'm in control now," I knew I was witnessing history. It was all part of the hysteria surrounding the day's events. Jim Brady, the White House press secretary, who was also severely wounded that day, was someone I worked closely with on a daily basis. It had hit very close to home. This tragic event, which took place only sixty-nine days after President Reagan had assumed office, became a defining moment for all of us. For me it was a sobering reminder about how ephemeral the exercise of power could be.

The rarified White House was a different place after March 30, 1981. A sadder and more somber place.

Thankfully, President Reagan was back at his desk very soon; 1981 was a big year for the president. He was there in time to meet with Avital Sharansky on May 28; to present the Robert F. Kennedy Jr. Congressional Medal to Ethel and Ted Kennedy on June 5; to host the annual White House Fourth of July picnic for staffers and their families; and to preside over a brilliant state dinner to honor Prime Minister Menachem Begin of Israel on September 9. I worked on some of the preparations for the Sharansky meeting and the Begin state dinner. They were personally gratifying and fulfilling events for me. Avital Sharansky made an impassioned plea to the president for her husband's release. As a result the president exerted intense pressure on the Soviet Union. Anatoly was finally freed in February 1986.

My White House appointment to the National Security Council presented some very real challenges for me. Dick Allen espoused a policy of minimal contact with the press. He called it the "low profile" National Security Council. He was very selective about the journalists he would talk to, and he avoided the Sunday talk shows like the plague. This policy made my job as press officer for the NSC very difficult and challenging. I had learned a lot from watching Jim Baker when he was the chief spokesperson for the Bush for President campaign in 1979. Baker was exceptionally adept at managing the Bush campaign's press corps. As he had done, I accepted every press phone call and tried to provide the reporters with tidbits of helpful information and quotes, as well as the names of other knowledgeable people who could be contacted. But I was rarely able to deliver Dick Allen. I developed a reputation as someone who would try to help the journalists write their stories. It was a feather in my cap. In Washington, you need the media to be on your side—or at least not out to get you.

In early August of 1981, the second Jerusalem Women's Seminar left for ten days in Israel and Egypt. Among the participants were myself, Ursula Meese, Helene von Damm, and Nancy Reynolds. After the JWS program ended, we accepted the invitation of Ambassador Ali and Mrs. Benjelloun of Morocco to visit their country. The Washington press corps was intensely curious about all aspects of our travel. The *Washington Post* published several gossipy articles describing a "White House travel junket" and a "propaganda mission by a pro-Israel staffer." I feared the worst. However, Dick Allen and Fred Fielding, White House general counsel, approved the trip, and we were good to go. We weathered the media storm and left for our Middle East adventure.

By the time we arrived in Casablanca, after ten days of intense dialogue and little sleep in Israel and Egypt, we were ready to be just ordinary tourists. That was not to be. The personal advisors to King Hassan of Morocco took charge of our visit. We received the royal treatment in Casablanca, Rabat, Marrakech, and Fez. In the royal hunting lodge in the town of Ifrane in the Atlas Mountains, we were hosted by the king in a typically colorful woven Berber tent under the stars. We finally arrived in Tangiers, where we stayed for a few days of rest and relaxation before returning to the United States. Malcolm Forbes invited us to stay in his palace. His famous miniature-soldier collection was on full display to keep us company.

Tangiers is a very special place. At a dinner hosted by the US consul general, we learned that the first US consulate in the Middle East, the oldest diplomatic property in the world and one of the most beautiful buildings in Tangiers, was established by President George Washington in 1797 as a "testament to the special nature of the U.S.-Moroccan relationship." Every minute of our visit to Morocco was unique and unforgettable. We returned to DC a few weeks before the official state visit of Prime Minister Menachem Begin of Israel. We had spent time with the prime minister while visiting Israel. We were much more knowledgeable about the region, and we well understood the challenges that lay ahead.

On a fall afternoon in 1981, Nancy Reagan hosted a tea for the senior White House women staffers. We changed into our party outfits in our offices and met in the East Room for the event at 4:00 p.m. There was a long receiving line. As I got closer to greeting Mrs. Reagan and having my picture taken, I realized I was wearing the identical David Hayes red wool suit that she was wearing. I didn't know what to do. I found myself standing and shaking in front of Mrs. Reagan and telling her, "You have very good taste in red suits." She barely smiled and motioned to the photographer not to take my picture with her. I tried to stay out of sight during the event from that moment on. I emerged unscathed. I would be more careful next time Nancy Reagan invited me to an event.

An ongoing battle over perks and privileges was an integral part of the White House scene. For example, Dick Allen did not allow me to have White House mess or parking privileges. His pithy, off-the-cuff comments directed at me also made me feel very uncomfortable in front of other NSC staff members, mostly male. I thought he was joking around and ignored his comments. I did not react to what were clearly provocative comments clearly intended to be funny, chalking it all up to the pressures of work and a weird sense of humor. I suffered in silence. Since, in many cases, I was the only woman in the room, his comments were interpreted by others as harassing and sexist. White House staffers who were present noticed and didn't like it, In fact, they were offended.

● ● ●

Months went by, and internal tensions inevitably emerged among senior administration officials. Dick Allen was having problems, although I could never be sure what they were. I knew that they were serious and that he would be leaving at some point. Iran-Contra was happening all around me, but I was, thankfully, out of the loop.

One day I received a call to come to the office of Chief of Staff James Baker. Since I was a member of Dick Allen's personal staff, I was prepared for the worst. I arrived for the Baker meeting on a snowy, gray day in December 1981. Mike Deaver and Ed Meese were also there. I was scared, and I'm sure they knew that. Seeing Ed Meese there made it a little better. He was a strong and comforting man who had always been very kind to me. And then those magic words came out of Jim Baker's mouth: "We have a job for you."

Things were looking up. When the time was right and White House senior staff members were contemplating staff changes, I was deliberately lifted out of the trouble zone and promoted to another high-level, visible position in the administration. Once again, my friends were there for me. My friends in the media also came through for me with favorable coverage of the move. That always helps in the DC power game.

Dick Allen did leave the White House shortly thereafter, in early January 1982. The media pilloried him. For them it was payback time.

By "luck and pluck," as the well-known novelist Judy Bloom would say, a couple of weeks later I found myself at another desk—this time at the United States Information Agency (USIA). I was promoted to the position of director of the Office of Public Liaison, which included the Voice of America broadcasting division.

I remember my high-school teacher asking each student what his or her preferred job would be after college. At the time, I responded unequivocally that I wanted to work for the Voice of America. Twenty-five years later, here I was. As I was the only woman in senior management at the agency, the director often referred to me as a "rose among thorns." Charlie Wick, the director, and Gil Robinson, the deputy director, were fun to work with. They were creative, funny, and dedicated. I felt close to Charlie and called him by his first name. He was a member of President Reagan's Kitchen Cabinet. I respected him but spoke up when I thought he was making an error in judgment on an issue. The rest of the senior staff tiptoed around him. I believe he respected me for being honest and forthright. I loved my dream job!

The timing was fortuitous. The challenges were historic. We were witnessing the beginning of the breakup of the Soviet Empire. President Reagan was determined to reach the people of eastern Europe through broadcasting. He stepped up funding for Radio Free Europe and Radio

Liberty to break through to the people in eastern Europe and Russia. The president also wanted to reach the people of Communist Cuba, and Radio Martí was established.

The Solidarity Movement in Danzig, Poland, led by Lech Walesa and the dockworkers, received a lot of our attention. Danzig was the city where my parents had boarded the ship *Lituania* on their escape to freedom in January 1930. Charlie Wick came up with the idea to create a short documentary titled *Let Poland Be Poland* for broadcast in Europe. The film was intended to encourage the strikers and the Polish people to continue their fight for freedom. It had a major impact all over eastern Europe. It was one of the crowning achievements of public diplomacy in the Reagan administration. The Berlin Wall came down soon after Reagan left office in 1989.

President Reagan realized the importance of public diplomacy and campaigned for more funding for these kinds of efforts. Under President Clinton the entire USIA structure, including the Voice of America, was folded into the State Department and the Board of International Broadcasting. The benefit of having America's voice heard around the world, especially in the Middle East, was significantly diminished. Our public-diplomacy efforts suffered a severe setback and have never fully recovered.

I was breaking down barriers along the way during my time at USIA. I received official approval to participate in the third Jerusalem Women's Seminar in 1982. The dream of the JWS was still alive, and I was determined to be part of it even though I was a government official. In 1983, I was the first woman ever to address the Harry S. Truman Presidential Foundation Annual Luncheon in Independence, Missouri. It seems laughable now, but at the time it was unprecedented.

President Reagan made a special effort to bring qualified women into his administration. He established a Presidential Personnel Task Force on Women. I was asked to help identify female candidates for high-level administration positions. The monthly meetings were held in the Roosevelt Room of the White House.

At one of the meetings, a White House staffer brought me a note asking me to stop at Bill Clark's office before leaving the White House. Bill Clark, or Judge Clark, as he was called, the man who succeeded Dick Allen as national-security advisor, was a friend and a Reagan advisor and confidante. I walked into his office with some trepidation and once again heard a familiar phrase. "Phyllis. The president has a job for you."

I had to find a seat quickly. I nervously said, "Bill, I have a wonderful job. I love my job."

Bill responded by saying once again, "The president has a job for you."

I had been around long enough to know what that meant. You listen when the president "has a job for you."

President Reagan chose me to become director of the United Nations Information Center in Washington—a senior position never before held by an American or a woman. It was the equivalent of the United Nations Embassy in the capital of the organization's largest contributor and most powerful member state.

I remember saying, "Bill, I'm not right for the job. I'm not a UN supporter."

And then he closed out the discussion by saying, "That's why the president wants you in this job."

I smiled and realized the discussion was over. As I left his office, Bill instructed me to fly to New York to be interviewed by Secretary-General Pérez de Cuéllar as soon as possible. I was in tears as I walked back to my USIA office on Pennsylvania Avenue. I tried to understand why I was being "exiled" to the UN. In my view, it was nothing less than a political graveyard. I thought that my luck had run out. I was being put out to pasture.

When I returned to my office that afternoon, I received a phone call from Ambassador Jeane Kirkpatrick's office with the details of the New York visit arranged for the next day. Before meeting with the secretary-general, I met briefly with Ambassador Kirkpatrick and then with her deputy, Ambassador Ken Adelman.

Ken's words were powerful. He said, "Phyllis, always remember where you came from. Don't allow yourself to be sucked into the bureaucracy of the UN and forget your American values and principles." I never did. Not once. Maybe that's why President Reagan or his advisors who knew me well selected me in the first place.

The next morning, as I was being escorted into the office of the secretary-general (SG), I still was not very enthusiastic about the whole thing. The SG was very warm and welcoming, and he asked me to tell him a little about myself. I had devised a plan on the flight up to New York. I would be completely truthful and sincere in the interview. I told Pérez de Cuéllar that I had grown up in New York City in the South Bronx, that I was a Republican, a woman of Jewish background, and a staunch supporter of the State of Israel. I was sure I had killed my chances of being approved for the position.

On the flight back, I was sure that I had flunked the interview. Much to my surprise, the next day Pérez de Cuéllar called Ambassador Kirkpatrick and told her that he liked my "honesty, integrity, and principled positions," rare qualities in the UN bureaucracy that he directed—a bureaucracy that had shown its anti-Israel stripes early on and had never promoted Jews to any senior position. My plan to be rejected for the UN position had backfired. A few weeks later, I reluctantly moved on to the next challenging chapter in my life as a high-level international civil servant.

THE DISUNITED NATIONS

It was April 1983. I was now the director of the United Nations Information Center in Washington, DC. I moved into the spacious offices of the United Nations Information Center (UNIC-DC) located next to the World Bank and the International Monetary Fund complex of buildings one block from the White House. My staff of fifteen were long-time UN employees well versed in the tricks of the trade. For me it was another learning experience. I had a feeling this new assignment would not be an easy one.

The first thing I did was personalize my surroundings. I hung Peruvian lithographs and Israeli artwork, used Islamic and Guatemalan toss pillows in our reception area, and placed Tunisian and Turkish rugs on the floor. The offices became a colorful, welcoming place. We were ready for visitors.

In retrospect, I had numerous encounters with the United Nations (UN). In 1959, while I was living in Geneva, Switzerland, I worked as an editor of the UN Disarmament Proceedings. In 1970 I was an official hostess on Mayor Lindsay's Committee for the Twenty-Fifth Anniversary Celebration of the UN in New York City. In 1982 President Reagan appointed me to serve as a US delegate to the UN Conference on the Rights of Women in Vienna, Austria. In 2003 I would serve as an official delegate to the UN Human Rights Council.

In my mind the organization had become something other than that envisioned by the original founders in 1945. By the time I joined the UN Secretariat in 1983, I was no longer a member of the UN fan club. With that in mind, it's clear that President Reagan picked the right person. I would not be bullied, nor would I give up my principles in order to be an international civil servant. The UN was a structurally flawed organization. Its founders hoped to prevent future world wars and genocides like the Holocaust. However, the dream we all hoped for has been derailed. The world has changed dramatically since 1945. But the UN has not changed to reflect the new reality of its majority membership from the developing world. It has become an organization where corruption is widespread. It has also become a giant boondoggle for the countries who are the least worthy. On a daily basis at the UN, totalitarian regimes trying to undermine and weaken democratic societies unleash a tide of hatred aimed at Israel and the West. In my mind, the UN has simply lost its way.

My journalist friend Claudia Rosett said it best in 2016: "The UN is packaged as an endless array of UN-orchestrated goals, capacity-building programs and bureaucratically directed spending of other people's money, much of it funneled through despotic governments whose oppressive misrule is the main reason for the poverty and perils the UN proposes to alleviate." She continued to say, "If all this sounds like the saga of a global mafia that happens to have acquired diplomatic immunity, plus an annual multibillion entitlement from US taxpayers, plus a luxurious headquarters complex in midtown Manhattan, plus a neo-colonial globe-girdling empire of offices, programs, staff, public-private partnerships, trust funds and influence, you've got the idea."

I had few illusions about the magnitude of the task I had been given—to improve and strengthen the working relationship between the United States and the United Nations. Many DC insiders told me that I was lucky to have landed a boondoggle appointment. All I knew was that I had been given the unenviable job of explaining the UN to a distrustful America and its skeptical government. It was nothing less than a diplomatic hot seat. Certain countries—Algeria, India, France, Pakistan—had become adept at playing the game at the UN. The United States and other Western countries were not among these countries. We played by the rules. The other countries did not. It was a constant battle.

Once again press coverage of my appointment as director of UNIC-DC was very well-received. Articles appeared in the *New York Times*, *National Journal*, *Washingtonian Magazine*, *Working Woman Magazine*, the *Washington Post*, the *Pittsburgh Press*, the *Johnstown Tribune*, and many others. The positive coverage continued throughout my time as a UN official. I also bylined numerous columns primarily about the UN and the humanitarian work of its specialized agencies (e.g., World Health Organization, UN Children's Emergency Fund (UNICEF), the UN Development Organization, and World Food Program).

I was very much in demand as a public speaker for civic organizations and academic groups across the country—Los Angeles, San Francisco, Tampa, Miami, Louisville, Princeton, Palm Beach, Altoona, Pittsburgh, Milwaukee, Columbus, Saint Paul-Minneapolis, Santa Barbara, Houston, Phoenix, and Dallas, to mention a few. I tried to be unbiased and supportive of the humanitarian work that the UN does around the world. However, I was openly critical of the political deception and geopolitical games that were played in the General Assembly and the Security Council. It did not take me long to learn about the bureaucratic shenanigans occurring at the UN on a daily basis. The audiences appreciated my frankness and honesty. My New York UN colleagues were not very happy.

Almost from the outset, I felt like I was viewed as an interloper and was quickly considered a renegade by UN officials in New York. I had a feeling that I would not last very long as the director in DC. Nevertheless, I was determined to fulfill my commitment to the president. I set out to learn the ropes and play a smart but productive game. When I arrived, UNIC-DC was a sleepy, off-the-radar entity that few in Washington had heard of or cared about. I decided to change that image and turn it into a social and political player on the Washington scene. I told the *New York Times* that for UN officials "there are so many things happening in Washington they don't understand."

I was very uncomfortable with the strict and restraining UN administrative guidelines. I rebelled against the language of political correctness that permeated the UN bureaucracy. I encountered more and more UN staff members less concerned with abiding by the ethical standards of the international civil service than with taking shortcuts and doing whatever was most convenient. From the beginning of my tenure, my maverick style was obvious. I know I raised a lot of eyebrows in Washington and New York. I was frequently mentioned and criticized by the UN press corps in New York at the daily UN press briefings. Let's just say I was not your ordinary UN official. They were watching me.

In August 1983, I went on the last Jerusalem Women's Seminar. A friend of mine, Walt Cutler, had been appointed US ambassador to Tunisia. He and his wife, Didi, invited me to visit as their guest at the ambassadorial residence after the seminar meetings. I took them up on the invitation and spent a very interesting few days with my wonderful hosts. The residence was located in a lovely suburb of Tunis (which used to be the Roman province of Carthage) with a magnificent view of the Mediterranean. Ambassador Cutler's neighbor across the street was none other than Yāsser Arafat, the head of the Palestine Liberation Organization. An eye-opener for me.

My New York colleagues wondered where in the Middle East I would turn up next. I didn't disappoint.

I created the UN Peace Medal, to be awarded annually on UN Day, October 24. The first medal was bestowed in 1984 on Mrs. Esther Coopersmith, a well-known Washington hostess who promoted dialogue and dinner among those who viewed the world from different vantage points. At her dinner parties, important views were exchanged among guests who came from the former Soviet Union, the Middle East, and Israel. The Coopersmith dinners were the talk of the town. She deserved recognition for her efforts to bring people together to share their views. Six hundred guests were treated to a magnificent reception and dinner in the Great Marble Hall of the Organization of American States. The media coverage was amazing. I had accomplished my first objective:

"I had put the United Nations on the map in DC," according to The Washington Post.

In 1985 I hosted a spectacular event at the World Bank to celebrate UN Day with Ken Kragen, president of USA for Africa, of "We Are the World" fame. The focus of the event was the UN's work in feeding and caring for those in need in Africa. Peter McPherson, USAID administrator at the time, was master of ceremonies. Hundreds of people were there as I presented the UN Peace Medal to Ken. We also sponsored a UN Day concert at Kennedy Center. The press loved it! My colleagues in New York liked this one.

In 1986 Dr. Allen Weinstein was awarded the UN Peace Medal. He was a well-known author and academic, the founder of the Center for Democracy. He was a champion in the world of democracy and the promotion of free elections. In 2005 he became the ninth archivist of the United States.

I raised the visibility of Secretary-General Pérez de Cuéllar in DC and gave him a positive presence in the corridors of DC power. I spent much of my time organizing visits to Washington for the secretary-general and many other senior UN officials eager to sell their wares to the Washington elites. I was widely complimented for my programming and entertaining skills in DC. Ed Derwinski, the State Department counselor, said, "In my judgment Phyllis has been the most effective Washington-based representative the UN has ever had." I knew how to throw a good party and turn out people from the Washington A-list. The word spread quickly to UN officials around the world. Sooner or later they showed up in DC requesting meetings with senior US officials and, of course, receptions as well.

The famed Soviet dissident, Anatoly Sharansky, was harshly imprisoned by the Soviet Union. This brave man was finally freed in February 1986. I sent him a congratulatory telegram in my UN capacity. On May 13, 1986, he came to Washington to thank all of us who had worked on his behalf. I arranged for him to address the National Press Club. It was a glorious, heartwarming occasion. This courageous man was now living in freedom in Israel. Again, my colleagues in New York were not as thrilled about my involvement in Sharansky-related events as I was.

In 1984 I attended the UN Conference on Population, held in Mexico City. The conference was very controversial. The abortion issue was front and center. The US government was prepared to boycott based on proposals promoting the use of foreign government funds to pay for abortions. In the end, the United States participated but announced a cutback in contributions to UN family planning programs to protest the use of foreign government funding for abortions. Since the 1970s, US law had explicitly prohibited the use of foreign assistance funds to pay for abortion services. President Bill Clinton reversed this policy, and it has become a political football ever since.

The 1984 conference was held at the Hotel Presidente in downtown Mexico City. Several times during my eight-day stay, I ventured out for a walk to see some of the tourist sites and get some fresh air. There was no fresh air to be had. I quickly returned to the hotel. The pollution was so overwhelming I was unable to breathe. I never left the hotel again except to go to the airport. I had dinner with an old friend, Moshe Arad, the Israeli ambassador to Mexico, at the restaurant in the hotel. I also met with some of Sam's relatives, who lived in Mexico City, at the hotel. I can't really say that I visited Mexico City. Too bad!

I traveled extensively to Middle East hot spots. Peacekeeping operations in the region were of special interest to me. In 1984 I toured the major UN peacekeeping sites in the Middle East on the Syrian and Israeli border (UNDOF), the Lebanese and Israeli border (UNIFIL), and, of course, Truce Supervision Operations (UNTSO) in Jerusalem. I was accompanied by General Brian Urquhart, a dashing British Royal Air Force general and director of UN peacekeeping operations. General Urquhart had arranged for us to fly into Beirut on UN aircraft, but it turned out to be too dangerous, and we turned back. While in Jerusalem I took the opportunity to meet with Israeli government officials, some of whom were personal friends. Jerusalem-based UN Truce Supervision and Observation (UNTSO) officials frowned upon my meetings with Israelis.

The peacekeeping troops from Canada, India, Austria, and Fiji were very warm and welcoming. They were especially pleased to have a visit from a female UN official to break the monotony of their isolated hill-top locations. The peacekeepers were well-meaning and well-informed. However, I detected the usual anti-Israel bias in the briefings by British and French officers and UN civilian personnel attached to the peace-keeping battalions.

In 1986 I undertook the European grand tour, visiting my counter-part directors in London, Paris, Rome, Vienna, and Geneva. Sam accompanied me on this trip. I was graciously wined, dined, and briefed by my fellow UNIC directors. I learned a lot about the internal politics of the various UNIC directors. It was all politics all the time in UN offices around the world.

My close friend, Helene von Damm, was the American ambassador in Vienna. The president had appointed her to serve in the country of her birth. We spent time together catching up on Washington gossip and eating Austrian pastries. A leading Jewish supporter of Ronald Reagan, Max Rabb, was the American ambassador in Rome. Max invited us to his residence for a dinner party being held to honor Leonard Bernstein, who was visiting Rome at the same time. My colleague Gerry Carmen was the US ambassador to the UN in Geneva. He hosted us at a dinner party and gave us a tour of his official residence.

Sam and I took a slight detour and added a few days in Monte Carlo to the itinerary. I had not been back to the principality since I left in 1970. Nothing much had changed. It was a place frozen in time sixteen years later. For me it was also a place filled with so many mixed memories.

While in Vienna I made a side trip to Budapest, Hungary, where I met up with my UNIC executive assistant, Zsolt Tzekeres. When Zsolt heard that I would be visiting Vienna, he offered to meet me there and escort me on a visit to his homeland. Nicolas Salgo, the former owner of the Watergate Hotel and a Reagan appointee, was our ambassador in Budapest. His official instructions were to meet with only recognized Hungarian government officials.

Ambassador Salgo invited me to tea at the embassy. I told him I would be bringing some Hungarian friends with me. Five of the leading Hungarian dissidents, who could never have dreamt of gaining entry to the US Embassy, came through the visitor's gate. And there they were, having tea with the American ambassador. Nick Salgo was gracious but somewhat taken aback at what I had done. Never mind. When the Berlin Wall came down in 1989, these dissidents joined the new democracy in free and democratic elections. I was proud of myself. I had done the right thing for the United States and Hungary. UN officials in New York were not happy.

After the grand tour, I returned to Washington and was told that Ambassador Carmen would be leaving his UN ambassadorial post in Geneva shortly. I informed the White House that I would be interested in succeeding him. I lined up references and supporters for the White House Presidential Personnel Office. Everyone agreed that I would be the perfect choice for the posting. But it was not to be. I came in second to Mr. Joseph Petrone, of Marshalltown, Iowa. Mr. Petrone was married to the heiress of the Sheraton Hotel fortune, a Republican Eagle, and a major financial supporter of the Republican Party. I was married to a then Democrat small-town family lawyer from Johnstown, Pennsylvania. A $100,000 contribution from the Kaminskys was not in the cards. Another political lesson learned the hard way.

On a Friday afternoon a few months later, I received a call from the White House Presidential Personnel Office. They had found the "perfect" embassy for me. My fluency in French was certainly part of their thinking. They asked if I would consider being the US ambassador to Haiti. Papa Doc Duvalier was in the last throes of his corrupt regime. There was hope that a new, democratic Haiti would emerge from the debris of decades of dictatorship. I thought about the offer over the weekend and mulled it over with Sam.

That Sunday I was visited in my home by Mr. Marc Bazin, a Haitian development economist at the World Bank, who was known as "Mr. Clean." He eventually became prime minister of Haiti. Bazin was viewed as pro-American and a respected proponent of stable democracy for his country. He urged me to accept the position. He promised to work closely with me to bring a better life to his people. Nevertheless, on that Monday I advised the White House that I could not accept the offer. I had a young child and a full-time lawyer husband. They did not want to live in Haiti. And I did not want to go to Haiti without them. However, for me Haiti will always be a special country. I often wonder if I could have made a real difference for the Haitian people. I also wonder how different my life would have been if I had carried the lifetime title of ambassador.

In 1987 I flew to Moscow on Aeroflot Airlines to participate in an international gathering of UN Information Center directors. The meeting took place at a time when resistance to Soviet rule was growing. We stayed at the Cosmos Hotel on Kremlin Square for several days. There were two burly Soviet guards seated outside of my hotel room 24-7. I asked our Soviet hosts if I could visit the city of Kaunas, the birthplace of my father, which was relatively close by in Lithuania. They turned me down with the excuse that Kaunas was a "closed military city." I requested that I be able to visit the Moscow synagogue. They turned me down again, this time with no excuse. The food was atrocious. I ate caviar, chicken broth, brown bread, and smoked salmon the entire time—morning, noon, and night. I lost seven pounds during my horrific stay in Moscow. It felt as if I were in prison. I vowed never to return.

During my time as UNIC director, I got to know many of Africa's up-and-coming diplomats, such as James Jonah of Sierra Leone and Doudou Diène of Senegal, who went on to become heads of state or senior ministers in their countries. The developing world viewed the UN as the best training ground for their future heads of state, prime ministers, and foreign ministers. They sent their most promising political leaders to serve as UN ambassadors in New York. I was their best contact in Washington. My UN Rolodex was growing.

The International Fund for Agricultural Development (IFAD), led by Director Idriss Jazairy of Algeria at the time, was a UN entity that I wholeheartedly endorsed. IFAD specialized in small loans to individuals and groups in the developing world, mainly women, to create entrepreneurship and income modeled on the well-known Grameen Bank formula started in Bangladesh. The agency worked well, free of corruption, and it was well administered. IFAD was one of the few winners!

Dr. Jazairy introduced me to Algeria's ambassador to the United States, Mahmoud Sahnoun. The ambassador invited me to a private dinner at his residence. An intriguing invitation! Once again, my French came in handy. The guests consisted of twenty high-level World Bank and Arab officials from various Washington embassies. I was the only woman. I sat between Ambassador Sahnoun and a senior World Bank official, who at any given moment was Egyptian, Kuwaiti, or Palestinian. He carried all three passports. Throughout the evening I was treated with great respect and dignity. The issue of Middle East politics never came up, even though the ambassador knew I was Jewish and considered to be pro-Israel. For him, this was strictly a UN event. And an unforgettable one at that! Ambassador Sahnoun remained a friend and supporter until I left the UN in 1988. He went on to become a senior UN envoy after completing his term in Washington.

I also had a good relationship with Israel's then ambassador to the UN, the current Prime Minister Benjamin Netanyahu, whom I met with several times over the five-year period I was at the UN. Once again, my New York colleagues looked askance.

Every year I went back to President Reagan's national-security advisor and the secretary of state to suggest that I had served my time at the UN and was ready to move on. Each time Secretary of State George Shultz and his deputy, John Whitehead, told me that the administration was very pleased with my performance, and I was asked to stay on. I admired Secretary Shultz more than any person I worked for in the Reagan administration. He was steady, solid, and forceful in his own quiet way. A number of contentious UN-related issues were raised during the Reagan administration. The controversies kept coming, one after another, and I was told I needed to see them through.

Phyllis Kaminsky

President Reagan decided that UNESCO (otherwise known as the United Nations Educational, Scientific and Cultural Organization) needed real reform. A founding member of UNESCO in 1948, the United States historically was its largest financial contributor. The United States contributed 25 percent of UNESCO's $180 million annual budget at the time of US withdrawal in 1984. President Reagan rightly determined that the organization had become politicized, corrupt, anti-West, and financially irresponsible. Our ambassador to UNESCO was withdrawn and funding withheld until a process of reform and change could be completed. Reform never happened. Instead UNESCO continues to be a political football.

Intense lobbying by UN supporters in the United States resulted in our conditionally rejoining UNESCO in September 2002 under the George W. Bush administration. We became full players again under President Obama. In 2015 the United States withheld its contribution to UNESCO because of congressionally mandated cuts due to UNESCO's recognition of Palestine as a member state.

The next UN crisis involved the extensive files about Nazi war crimes found in the UN's original post–World War II military archives at the headquarters building in New York City. The files revealed that Kurt Waldheim, the previous secretary-general, who served from 1972 to 1982, was a former German SS officer. He was identified as directly complicit in Nazi military operations that led to the destruction of the Jewish community in Salonika, Greece, as well as in the execution of anti-Nazi fighters in western Bosnia. When the story broke, I was seated at my desk located next to a wall of photographs of all the UN secretaries-general since 1945. Kurt Waldheim's photograph was among them.

My first reaction was mostly shock. My second reaction was fury. I requested that the office manager remove the picture immediately. I could not live with a former Nazi looking over my shoulder every day. Word traveled quickly back to New York. My skeptical colleagues in New York did not see the issue the same way I did. There were few to no other

Jews in the UN's senior leadership anywhere in the world. I was it! The Waldheim revelations were another nail in the coffin of the vaunted UN organization. I could not stomach a former secretary-general who was an active Nazi. I stuck to my guns. His picture would not hang on my office wall.

After his term at the UN, Kurt Waldheim went on to be elected president of Austria in 1986. A stunning development for me! He finally died in 1988, after having been rehabilitated by the voters of Austria less than forty years after the end of World War II. Kurt Waldheim perpetrated the most elaborate political deception of our time. For me the term "never again" lost its meaning after this experience at the UN.

Still another crisis was the opening of an unofficial Palestine Liberation Office (PLO) information office in New York in 1964. A serious attempt was made by the U.S. Congress and various Jewish groups to close down the PLO office following the passage of the US Anti-Terrorism Act in December 1987, which proclaimed the PLO a terrorist organization. Various courts in the United States ruled against this action but ultimately allowed for stricter supervision of the office's activities. The PLO issue caused great difficulty for the United States for many years. It was a constant problem for me and my staff in DC.

In an effort to promote UN reform and lessen corruption, Congress passed legislation to cut off or reduce funding to the UN, its specialized agencies, and its peacekeeping operations. The possibility of a financial cutoff was ever present during the five years I served. Implementation of the Kassebaum and Lugar amendments was a constant threat to UN funding.

There were also numerous Congressional attempts to withhold funding for the UN's closing conference on the Decade for Women in Nairobi in 1985. By that time the UN had become so politicized and anti-West that UN-sponsored conferences had become nothing more than international platforms for the perpetrators of human rights abuses, anti-Americanism, and anti-Semitism. These costly gatherings had become counterproductive.

Phyllis Kaminsky

I knew that I had caused the secretary-general and his staff considerable grief and anguish. For me five years at the UN was comparable to twenty-five years anywhere else. It was taking its toll on me as well. I decided it was time to move on. By March 1988, after repeated visits to the White House asking to be relieved of this assignment, I took the matter into my own hands. I flew to New York, met with the secretary-general, and handed in my resignation. I was planning to get involved in the George H. W. Bush 1988 campaign and, therefore, could not continue as a "nonpartisan" international civil servant. In many ways he was surprised and relieved. He knew in his heart that it was time. He was a gentlemen and a statesman until the last day. He told me that senior UN officials rarely resign. Life is too good to voluntarily give up all the perks and prestige that come with the job. However, in my mind the UN was well on its way to irrelevance.

For me it was time to leave this frightening universe dominated by third-world dictatorships and petty politicized bureaucrats. The UN is a community of 193 member states (110 of which are Muslim majority nations), of which the majority are not free. They have zero accountability to the people they supposedly represent. The Kim dynasty of North Korea is a member, but the free and democratic republic of Taiwan has not been accepted for membership. I left the UN in March 1988, exactly five years to the date of my original appointment to the position. When I left, my UN Rolodex was bulging with high-level contacts all over the world. Time to put it to work. Time to try something else. Time to start over one more time.

In 1988 I established an international consulting and strategic-planning company based in DC. My Rolodex served as my calling card in my transition to the private sector. The five long years as part of the UN bureaucracy had not all been for naught!

As politics would have it, my resignation was not the end of my UN experience. Five years later on March 17, 2003, I arrived in Geneva, Switzerland, as a delegate to the UN Human Rights Commission. Ambassador Jeane Kirkpatrick was brought back to chair our delegation after her resignation as UN ambassador in 1985. I was honored to be asked to serve by President George W. Bush. It was well-known in DC that I knew how the UN works. However, I was not privy to the information that the US invasion of Iraq would begin two days after our arrival in Geneva. Our delegation walked straight into the lion's den.

The US delegation was seated in the conference hall between France and Cuba. The chairperson of the fifty-ninth session was a woman from Libya. The verbal attacks came at us fast and furious on March 19, even from countries I call our "dishonest allies."

When the United States is condemned for human rights violations by UN ambassadors from Cuba, China, Russia, Libya, Sudan, Zimbabwe, and Saudi Arabia, you scratch your head in disbelief. You ask yourself, "What are we doing here? Has the world gone mad?" It seemed to me that by being there we had become an unwilling party to the name calling, hypocrisy, and mendacity that characterized most UN debates. At the end of every session, I rushed back to my hotel room to watch the battlefield news from Iraq on Swiss television. And then I could not sleep. It was a harrowing experience for the entire delegation.

The only good thing about the six-week Geneva assignment was the opportunity to spend almost every evening at dinner with Ambassador Kirkpatrick, a woman I admired and respected enormously. In 1981 President Reagan appointed her even though she was a well-known Democrat. While she was the US ambassador to the UN, she had famously told the president that she would take down the "kick-me sign" and that "we won't apologize." In 2003 she led the Geneva delegation on a valiant fight, responding to daily attacks on the United States. The United States was greatly outnumbered, and we had to fight for every vote from our so-called allies and friends.

Ambassador Kirkpatrick was extraordinarily adept at handling UN challenges. She did it with strength and commitment, although the United States was constantly on the defensive. I remember the Saudi Arabian ambassador in Geneva coming up to Ambassador Kirkpatrick to apologize for voting to condemn the US invasion of Iraq. He said, "I'm sorry. I'm sure you will understand. I had to vote against the US."

This statement, in a nutshell, is the way of life in UN bodies. There's a difference between what our so-called allies say in public and what they tell us in private behind closed doors. Sadly, events on the battlefield overtook progress on human rights issues. Not much was accomplished, and we were all glad the phony masquerade was over and we could go home.

THE FALL OF THE WALL
The Democracy Dividend

November 1989 ushered in major change in the world. It all happened very quickly. The United States was caught by surprise. The Berlin Wall came down. Almost overnight, the people of eastern Europe and central Asia were finally free after fifty years of Nazi and Soviet subjugation. More than fifteen countries were suddenly masters of their own fate. Americans were anxious to help these countries obtain a taste of freedom. I was part of that effort. I called it the democracy experiment. The results of this experiment are still not conclusive.

The nineties roared in a couple of months later. It was a decade of profound excitement as well as great danger. We witnessed massive positive change coupled with violence and brutality. Dark forces were also at work on the European continent. We were unprepared.

As we usually do, Americans embarked on the post-Soviet era with great optimism, outright joy, and a smattering of naïveté. I was no longer an international civil servant official. I was free to join in the celebration of freedom and be part of the real world, leaving the hypocrisy of the UN behind me.

Washington quickly created new organizations to fill the need. Think tanks responded first. Free elections were the top priority. American political consultants of all stripes were anxious to provide their expertise. Europeans were flying to Washington. Americans were flying to Warsaw, Prague, and Budapest. The tools of democracy and political-party training were shared. It was an inspiring and almost frenetic time. The fall of the Berlin Wall in 1989 had opened up the floodgates to a period of chaotic and awesome challenges.

In our rush to help emerging democracies, we may have lost sight of the fact that it would take multiple election cycles and many conferences and training sessions to achieve meaningful progress and reform. Democracy is hard. Change does not come easily or quickly to those who have grown accustomed to an authoritarian way of life.

People in the newly freed countries were not sure it was for real. They were uncertain and afraid. They needed to form new political parties. Party workers needed to be trained. The press had to adjust to printing the truth. The entire political and electoral system had to be overhauled. Sadly, to some countries, mainly in Muslim central Asia, democracy may never come.

It was January 1990. I was appointed to the Board of Directors of the International Republican Institute (IRI) by the chairman of the Republican Party, Lee Atwater. Other board members included Jeb Bush, Jack Kemp, Senator Richard Lugar, Ed Rollins, Frank Fahrenkopf, and Ambassador Jeane Kirkpatrick. The IRI was one of the preeminent democracy-promotion organizations. It was an incubator for the development of strategies and ideas to deal with the new post-Soviet political order. The National Democratic Institute (NDI) operated in a similar fashion for the Democratic Party. It was truly a bipartisan undertaking. I found myself in the thick of all this activity.

Many political junkies thought Lee Atwater to be one of the most hard-hitting political strategists ever. For me Lee was a gracious southern gentleman. He was someone who respected loyalty. He kept his promise to reward those who had toiled in the vineyards for the party, which made him a unique political operative—a reliable one. He was also irreplaceable after his untimely death in 1991. The IRI appointment was a gift to me at just the right time. It opened up vast new avenues of access and visibility for me in DC and made it easier to get new clients for Kaminsky Associates.

My appointment to IRI was fortuitous and ironic at the same time. My view of the world was shaped by my parents' escape from eastern Europe in the 1930s in search of freedom from persecution and anti-Semitism. I had clear memories of my parents' struggle to make a new life for themselves, first in Canada and then in the United States. Now sixty years later I became part of an extraordinary effort to bring freedom to those very countries my parents had escaped from. I worked hard for a number of years to help various eastern European countries throw off the yoke of communism even though some of those same countries - were complicit with the Nazi regime during WWII. It was the right thing to do in 1990 but I found it to be bitterly ironic for me personally.

In June 1990 I was a member of the official election-monitoring delegation to Czechoslovakia. Senators John McCain and Chris Dodd led the bipartisan delegation. Madeleine Albright, a future secretary of state, was on the delegation as well. For some reason, the first lady of Honduras, Norma Callejas, a former Miss Honduras, was also with us. Her presence garnered an inordinate amount of attention from the two senators. It struck me and others in the delegation as strange. The other delegation members questioned the value added.

It was inspiring to meet Václav Havel, the famed Czech dissident and playwright and soon to be freely elected president of the country. He was a short, soft-spoken man who had a reputation for toughness and determination. The Czech Republic (after splitting from Slovakia) became the first post-Soviet success story. Democracy had been part of their history in the thirties. The Czechs were anxious to go down that road once again.

I returned to Hungary as part of a political training mission in the mid-1990s. Some of the anti-Communist dissidents I met during my previous visit in 1986 as a UN official had indeed become part of the new political system. I conducted some media training and party strategy workshops with them. They were young, energetic, and excited about their new opportunity. Hungary's history was a checkered one, and it would become a work in progress for many years. Its bitter fight with Romania over the province of Transylvania continues to reverberate until this day.

Even more ironic, I assumed the Yugoslavia Portfolio on the IRI Board. You may remember that my first husband, Janez Hacin, was born in Slovenia, the smallest republic in former Yugoslavia. In the early nineties, after President Tito died, the various pieces of Yugoslavia, which he had held together by virtue of his strong, charismatic personality and authoritarian regime, began to break off. Events in the rest of Europe were spreading like a contagious fever across the entire continent. Little by little it became clear that Serbia, Croatia, Slovenia, Montenegro, Bosnia-Herzegovina, and Macedonia would eventually become independent states. Unlike the change in the rest of Europe, the breakup of Yugoslavia would be bloody, violent, and destructive.

Slovenia, the smallest of the republics, with a population of two million, became free first, after a brief ten-day insurgency against Serbia. Slovenia's elections were well run and somewhat hopeful. Croatia and Serbia would engage in a bitter, ugly war, which included the US bombing of Belgrade to force Serbia into submission. Bosnia, the Muslim-majority country, would become embroiled in an interreligious bloodbath that would last for several years.

I led the official US delegations that monitored the first free elections in Serbia, Croatia, and Bosnia. During 1990 and 1991, I traveled to former Yugoslavia fourteen times for elections and training sessions. Strangely enough, the elections were conducted fairly and without much violence. I was soon to realize that Communists were very proficient in conducting what they called "free and fair elections." I also learned the hard way that the government provided translators who told us only what they wanted us to hear and not what was really being said.

•   •   •

During a postelection briefing session with President Franjo Tudjman of Croatia, an unrepentant dictator who had been reelected in a so-called free election in 1991, one of the members of my delegation, Mira Ricardel, who was Croatian-American and spoke Croatian fluently, offered to take over the translator's job. I was finally able to get an accurate read-out on Mr. Tudjman. The bottom line was that he had been a Communist the day before. But now he had put on a different suit and called himself a Democrat. Tudjman was dishonest and unworthy of our trust and support.

Mira became one of my closest personal friends because of our shared experience in Croatia and also Bosnia. At the time she was the foreign-policy advisor to Senator Robert Dole, the Senate majority leader.

The postelection briefing in Belgrade, Serbia, was similar but more frightening. Newly reelected President Slobodan Miloševi was an old-style baby-faced Communist thug with an evil smile. He and his beefy bodyguards filled the room. He brooked no opposition and obviously had dangerous plans for the other entities that were preparing to declare their independence. He would never be a Democrat. We would hear more from him in the months and years to come. He eventually ended up in The Hague charged with war crimes, and he died in prison. We learned hard lessons in Croatia and Serbia. Slobodan Miloševi and Franjo Tudjman had both been resoundingly reelected in supposedly free and fair elections after the dissolution of Yugoslavia. Neither of them had any intention of moving forward democratically.

After the elections in Croatia, I decided to go to Slovenia and con-gratulate the newly elected president, Milan Kučan. I had never been there and was curious. Upon my arrival it was clear that the Slovenian authorities had done their homework. They knew everything about my Slovenian connection by marriage. Janez's family members were still very prominent and active. In fact, as I would learn several years later, the movers and shakers in Slovenia all knew each other. It was a gossipy place filled with petty political intrigue and second-guessing. Nevertheless, I met some wonderful, gracious people who welcomed me warmly.

● ● ●

Janez had a close childhood friend, Zarko Petan, a dissident play-wright and theater director who had been imprisoned under Tito's regime. Zarko had visited us in Geneva several times. He wrote a play, titled *Café Astoria*, about a college-student in the university town of Maribor and a Slovene and his American wife. The narrative closely paralleled the story of my marriage to Janez. I wanted to see Zarko. I had his address. I showed up at his building and rang the doorbell. There was no answer. So I sat on the stairs and waited for about thirty minutes. After a short time, Zarko came home. He was genuinely shocked to see me sitting there. We both started hugging and crying. I was able to spend a few hours with him and his wife in their apartment. I never saw him again. He passed away in May of 2014.

Newly elected President Milan Kučan of Slovenia was the most genuine person I met during my Yugoslav adventure. We became friends. He invited me to visit Slovenia as the guest of his new government as soon as I could return. Slovenia is a beautiful little country of two million people that has an ancient history of democracy. Slovenes are proud to tell you about their first brief run at democracy in the twelfth century with the installation of the dukes of Carinthia. Slovenia has struggled to retain its identity while being hemmed in by the Julian Alps and the Adriatic Sea. In 1990 it received another chance at democratic rule. This time the Slovenians did not hesitate to grab the brass ring. Slovenia is another success story.

A couple of years later, I did accept President Kučan's invitation to visit as the official guest of the government. I told Janez, David's father, about my proposed visit. He arranged to be in Slovenia at the same time. President Kučan arranged for me to stay in the Villa Podroznik, a magnificent villa that had been Tito's residence in previous times. When Janez pulled up to the residence in a small Volkswagen car to pick me up for dinner, I could tell he was extremely impressed and somewhat taken aback. He must have been asking himself, "How did this happen?" His little Zippy (his nickname for me) was an official guest of the president of his homeland, staying at Tito's former residence. Janez arranged for his whole family to meet for dinner that night for an unforgettable family reunion at a well-known Slovenian restaurant. Even though Janez and

I had been divorced since 1966, our presence together in a now democratic and free Slovenia was very special and memorable. I think about that extraordinary evening often. I admit to getting very sentimental about that get-together. After all, Janez was the father of my son, David, who had followed in his father's footsteps by attending Princeton and becoming a successful architect in America.

A few years later, I toured Slovenia with Sam as a private citizen. I wanted to share it with Sam as well. We toured the small country from top to bottom, from Portorož on the Adriatic to a spa in Murska Sobota, on the Hungarian border, the hometown of President Kučan. We wandered the streets of the Old City of Ljubljana, visited the Lipizzaner horse farm, spent a few days at a spectacular Lake Bled hotel, and toured the university town of Maribor, which was the setting of Zarko Petan's play *Café Victoria*. I introduced Sam to President Kučan and some of the wonderful Slovenes I had met over the years. More to come on my Slovenian adventures in the next chapter.

The road to independence for Bosnia was rocky and ugly. Mira and I continued to work together to help the Bosnians gain support in DC in the early nineties. Senator Dole was finally able to pass legislation to lift the arms embargo so Bosnia had a fighting chance against the Serbs and Croats. They were destroying Bosnia in the hopes of eventually dividing it between themselves. In Bosnia, ethnic divisions were deeply and bitterly ingrained among the Serbian Orthodox, Catholics, secular Muslims, and the small number of Jews who still lived there. It was painful to watch quasi-Nazi tactics return to central Europe once again. A number of my Bosnian colleagues suggested that the Muslims in Bosnia were suffering a fate similar to that of European Jews in the 1930s and 1940s. This of course had an immediate impact on me. Two small misunderstood peoples that shared a history of great suffering.

Mira and I worked closely with then Prime Minister Haris Silajdzic and then Bosnian Ambassador in Washington, Sven Alkalaj, to support the Dayton Accords, which finally halted the bloodshed. We traveled to Bosnia several times in the early nineties. It was stunning to witness

Europe's weakness and its unwillingness to confront brutality so soon after the end of World War II. Many regional experts in the United States even viewed the events in Bosnia as bordering on genocide by the Serbs. It was left to the United States to take action and for the UN peacekeepers to come in afterward. Whatever idealism I still may have had at that time disappeared completely because of what I saw and experienced in the heart of Europe in the early nineties in Bosnia and Croatia.

As happens frequently to political organizations in DC, the IRI board eventually went through some changes. The chairman, Senator McCain, was contemplating a future run for the presidency in 2000. He changed the composition of the board to reflect that ambition and the changing national-security situation. The nominations of Larry Eagleburger, former secretary of state, and General Brent Scowcroft, former NSC advisor, were brought to the board for a vote.

My Yugoslav experience led me to disagree with the appointment of Mr. Eagleburger, a former US ambassador to Yugoslavia. I was well aware of his consistent support of and past friendship with President Slobodan Miloševi of Serbia. I voted against his appointment. I was the sole vote against. Forty-eight hours later I received a letter from Senator McCain advising me that my term of board service was over. It was a hard lesson learned. I had bucked the IRI chairman, Senator McCain, and paid the price. Ambassador Jeane Kirkpatrick and Ambassador Rich Williamson came to my support, but McCain's decision would prevail. For him it was his way or the highway. He brooked no opposition to his choice. When McCain did eventually run for president in 2008, Larry Eagleburger and Brent Scowcroft were his top foreign-policy advisors.

A few years later, in 1996, President Clinton named me to serve on a little-known congressionally funded presidential commission. The commission had a cumbersome name, but its work was significant and meaningful. The US Commission for the Preservation of America's Heritage Abroad was created by one of my favorite members of Congress, former Representative Ben Gilman of New York. Congress established a fund to enable the preservation and restoration of synagogues, churches, cemeteries, and monuments that were destroyed or damaged in World War II. The primary focus was on countries in eastern Europe that were involved in the Holocaust in one way or another.

At my request, the commission, along with other groups, raised funds to rebuild the Jewish cemetery and synagogue in Sarajevo, Bosnia. During the war in the early nineties, the fiercest military exchanges in the Sarajevo area were fought across the tombstones of the old Jewish cemetery. The Serbs used their elevated hilltop location to fire down on defenseless Bosnian civilians in the city. The cemetery, the oldest in southeastern Europe, was directly in the line of fire. It became a casualty of the war. Funds were raised, and it has since been rebuilt and restored.

I was named cochair of the US-Slovenia Joint Cultural Heritage Commission. In 1996 I was the featured speaker at the Church of Saint Cyril in New York to celebrate the eightieth anniversary of its founding. Over the years I had become something of a celebrity in Slovenia and among Slovenian-Americans.

During my time as a commissioner, the United States entered into a bilateral cultural cooperation agreement with the newly independent country of Lithuania, my father's birthplace. I was asked to sign the agreement on behalf of the US government at the Lithuanian Embassy in DC. My husband, Sam, and our son Glenn were in the audience. The Lithuanian ambassador asked me to make some remarks. It was a very emotional moment for me. I tried to calm myself by looking at Sam and Glenn. I started by talking about the refusal of Soviet authorities to allow me to visit Lithuania as a UN official when I was in Moscow. I talked about my father's family and the pogroms that brought about the death of my father's youngest brother, Abraham. I mentioned the heartbreak of my grandmother Faige, for whom I was named. I talked about how frightening it must have been to be a Jew living in prewar Lithuania. I ended with the story of my father's family and their escape to freedom. I was in tears by the time I stopped speaking, as were others in the room. I was crying when I signed the treaty. Even though he was no longer alive, I know my father was crying as well.

Move Over Guys - Up, Up and Away

In late 1988 I formed an international consulting firm, Kaminsky Associates, based in DC. I was lucky. My timing was great.

Shortly afterward, in January 1989, I received a call from Ron Kaufman in Presidential Personnel at the White House. I went to meet with him, and he, once again, used a familiar phrase: "The president has a job for you." He told me that President Bush (the forty-first president) would like me to serve as the first civilian woman on the Board of Visitors (BOV) at the US Air Force Academy (USAFA)—a very prestigious and sought-after position.

I told Ron that neither I nor my family had any military background. I asked him if he was sure that I was the right person for this appointment. He then told me that the White House wanted a serious and strong professional woman for the position. The issue of sexual harassment at all the US military academies had emerged as a serious problem, especially at the Air Force Academy. My appointment would send a clear and direct message to female cadets. They would now have someone on the BOV to consult with, to confide in, and to trust. I accepted and welcomed the awesome responsibility. The sexual harassment issue in the military has become a singularly important concern for our country. It was important that we set an example for the other US military academies, at West Point and Annapolis.

Other members of the bipartisan BOV were retired high-ranking military officers and members of both houses of Congress. The revered former Senator Barry Goldwater was the long-time chairman. The board met four times a year at the Colorado Springs location of the US Air Force Academy. Many of the board members had daughters. They were anxious to see progress. They wanted to expand opportunities for their daughters. The sexual harassment issue hit them hard. They had a personal stake in dealing with the problem. They all cared deeply about what was happening at the academy, but they were not sure what they could do. I believe my presence and input helped bring the issue into perspective.

In 1991 I flew to Colorado Springs for an academy commencement ceremony on a Pentagon jet reserved for the air force secretary. President Bush was the featured speaker. I ended up sitting alone for several hours as a passenger in a sleek, seemingly windowless airplane. Merrill "Tony" McPeak, secretary of the air force, was flying the plane.

I was seated next to Chairman Barry Goldwater on the commencement dais. When the ceremony was over, President Bush got up to leave. The Secret Service followed him. As the president walked by me, he grabbed my arm and said, "Come with me, Phyllis." I jumped up and asked about my luggage. The president said, "Don't worry, Phyllis; your bags will be taken care of."

The next thing I knew, I was on the Marine One helicopter and then on Air Force One with President and Barbara Bush. The senior leadership of the National Security Council, including, of course, Brent Scowcroft, the national-security advisor, were waiting for us when we boarded the plane. It was my first time on Air Force One. The other staffers were regular flight passengers. I was sure this would be a once-in-a-lifetime experience for me. I gathered up everything in sight, from matchbooks to napkins, to take back as souvenirs for the family. The private and unforgettable meeting with the president and Barbara in their cabin during the flight was an unexpected treat. A few days later, the White House sent me souvenir photos of me with the president on Air Force One; those were the icing on the cake. Proximity to power can be infectious as well as intimidating!

With George H. W. Bush's loss of the presidency and the arrival of the Clinton administration, Washington changed dramatically for me.

Phyllis Kaminsky

On Inauguration Day, January 21, 1992, I received a phone call from the still Bush White House advising me that my seat on the BOV of the USAFA would be given to General Brent Scowcroft, Bush's now former national-security advisor. He was the same Brent Scowcroft whom I encountered many times in similar situations. Scowcroft kept popping in and out of my life. He was always stiff competition for me to take on. I was heartbroken, but I resigned as requested. I had matured and now understood exactly how the political game was played.

The Air Force Academy position was a great experience! Sam and I attended some exciting Navy-Air Force football games in Annapolis and Colorado Springs. We met many wonderful people who served our country with honor and commitment. When my time ended at the academy, I was satisfied that I had done my part in assisting and comforting the female cadets. Sexual harassment issues would be dealt with seriously from that point on and well into the future.

The USAFA appointment opened up a whole new world for me—the world of the military and aerospace. It was a new career that I would pursue for more than twenty-five years, and it presented many challenges and also many rewards. Kaminsky Associates became a serious and respected player in the defense industry, specializing in the Middle East, with a particular focus on Israel, Egypt, and Turkey. These countries were major international customers for US defense companies, and they were of strategic importance to the United States. I concentrated on political analysis, diplomatic outreach, and marketing strategy for my defense-industry clients. It was an exciting time for me, lasting well into the twenty-first century.

The nineties made up the era of the so-called Peace Dividend. Our primary enemy, the Soviet Union, was breaking up. At the same time, US defense companies were eager to grow their international markets.

On a visit to Johnstown to see Sam in late 1989, I met with Representative John P. Murtha Jr., or Jack, as we called him, a Democrat representing the congressional district of Pennsylvania, which included Johnstown.

Sam managed Jack's campaign for Congress in February 1974, a special election, which ended in a grueling vote recount. He was also the personal attorney and close friend of the Murtha family for many years. Jack survived the 1974 election by a slim margin and went on to serve for thirty-six years, until his untimely death in 2010. He was the longest-serving congressman from the state of Pennsylvania and the first Vietnam War marine veteran to be elected to Congress. He helped the western Pennsylvania area get back on its feet after the 1977 flood. He brought defense-industry investments of over $100 million a year to the area. He brought badly needed jobs to a depressed region. For his commitment to their region, the people of southwestern Pennsylvania revered and honored Jack. He eventually became the ranking member of the Defense Appropriations Subcommittee in the House and chairman when the Democrats were in control in 1989. He was one of the most powerful men in Washington. He relished every minute of it. Many Washington insiders considered him to be one of the "Seven Cardinals" of Congress. He controlled the budget of the Pentagon, the largest agency of the US government.

At our meeting Jack asked me what I had been doing since I left the UN in mid 1988. I told him I had done consulting work with a legal firm; account management with a well-known NY PR firm; and preparation of an in-depth proposal for the government of Taiwan, laying out a path for them to attain full-fledged UN membership.

I mentioned the Air Force Academy appointment that I had accepted just a few days earlier. Suddenly Jack's face lit up. He also said the magic words: "Give me a couple of days. I may have a job for you." I knew that very few people in DC turned Jack down if he called. A week later Bill Smith, vice-president of human resources at the General Dynamics Corporation (GD), telephoned with the good news. I had my first major consulting client. GD may have thought they were doing Jack a favor. They realized very soon afterward that I was a valuable asset for General Dynamics, a giant in the industry. All I needed was an introduction, and I was off and running.

Phyllis Kaminsky

I had gained entry into the defense and aerospace industry—a mostly male-dominated sector. I found my niche and put my international Rolodex contact list to work immediately. My first consulting assignment at GD was to work with Pakistani Ambassador Abida Hussain about the congressionally imposed delay in the delivery of F-16 fighter jets to her country. The sale had been held up by Congress because Pakistan had gone nuclear. GD believed it was time for the United States to deliver the planes Pakistan had ordered and paid for. Abida and I became good friends. I practically lived at her embassy for many months. We received a Texas-sized welcome when we visited Fort Worth together to see the F-16 assembly line. We developed comprehensive strategy to work with Congress. The team I worked with at GD had been given a difficult task. Congress would not cooperate. We failed.

Abida and I became close friends. She invited me to visit Pakistan as her guest. As much as I admired her, her husband, and her two lovely daughters at Harvard, I was wary of making the trip. Pakistan is a complicated country for Americans to visit and understand. My colleagues at GD often joked that my tombstone would say, "She never gave up trying to get the F-16s to Pakistan."

My time at GD was exemplary. It's a great company, and I worked with the best of them: Bill Anders, Jim Mellor, Hank Sechler, Gordon England, Mike Wynn, and many more. Eventually, Gordon went to the Pentagon as deputy secretary, and Mike became undersecretary for acquisition and secretary of the air force. I was always treated with great respect. My advice and recommendations were valued. These men would continue to be supportive of me for many years to come. Gordon England and Mike Wynne made sure I didn't get lost in the upcoming shuffling of cards in the defense industry. This experience taught me that women should not believe that they can always do it on their own. Very often we need men, and we should not resist their help when it is offered. A cooperative effort is usually more successful.

My next assignment was to work with GD Land Systems and the Turkish military to convince them to buy M-1 Abrams tanks. The Turks insisted on a transfer of US tank technology. I traveled to Turkey at least thirty times over the years. I learned a lot about their political system and military procurement issues. I also developed personal friendships with some of the top military leaders of Turkey. On one occasion I flew to Izmir, Turkey, on the GD corporate jet with CEO Mellor. At the end of the day, the Turks decided against buying our tank.

GD was also very supportive of the USAFA. During my term on the BOV, GD established a permanent chair at the academy in honor of William Anders, former astronaut and former CEO of the company. The USAFA and GD welcomed my efforts in this regard. I was honored to represent GD and be part of the dedication ceremony in Colorado Springs.

In 1991 the Bush 41 campaign asked me to serve on the Middle East Advisory Committee during his campaign for president. Another political campaign was in full swing. I was part of election excitement once again. As a consultant I was now free to be politically involved. My enthusiasm was short-lived. Sadly, this campaign ended in defeat. That was a new experience for me. I was used to winning.

In the meantime, the defense industry was in flux. Mergers and acquisitions were occurring more frequently. Senior executives were moving from one company to another. They all knew each other. It was a tight-knit circle. In the early nineties, GD, my first big client, embarked upon a period of restructuring and divestment.

GD sold Space Systems to Martin Marietta in 1994. They sold their Fort Worth division to Lockheed Corporation in 1993. The sale of the Fort Worth division had a direct impact on my consulting contract with GD. As a result, I became a consultant to the Lockheed Corporation.

Dan Tellep was the chairman and CEO of Lockheed at the time. I had the honor of introducing Mr. Tellep at a five-hundred-guest JINSA (Jewish Institute for National Security Affairs) dinner in late 1993. During our dinner conversation, I told Mr. Tellep, "It looks like I will now be working with Lockheed Fort Worth."

He turned to me and said, "You're worth at least one point five billion," the price paid by Lockheed to acquire GD Fort Worth. We both laughed. I felt very honored by his comments.

After his introduction, Chairman Tellep presented the Henry M. Jackson Leadership Award to none other than Jack Murtha, the congressman from Johnstown. It was clear to Jack that he had made a good decision one snowy day in Johnstown. I had not let him down.

I joined the JINSA(Jewish Institute for National Security Affairs) Board of Advisors in 1995. JINSA was founded to support a strong American defense capability and to promote American security with like-minded democracies, including Israel. JINSA was the perfect fit for me. As part of JINSA delegations, I traveled to Israel and Turkey extensively during the next decade.

As a result of the various mergers and acquisitions, Kaminsky Associates ended up having multiple consulting contracts with GD Land Systems, GD Electric Boat Company, Lockheed Corporation Fort Worth, GD Commercial Space Systems, and Martin Marietta Astronautics. Things were going very well. As years passed I ended up working solely with Lockheed Martin Corporation after Lockheed acquired Martin Marietta in 1995. It all sounds confusing, and it was. But it worked out well for me.

For many years I worked on the Lockheed Martin F-16 programs—the NATO fighter jet. In March 1996 Lockheed Martin decided to take advantage of my excellent contacts in Slovenia. I traveled there to meet with my old friend President Kučan and Slovenian defense officials about the possible purchase of a squadron of F-16 jet fighters.

The timing of my visit was problematic. The country was still suffering from a leftover Balkan and Communist mentality. I walked into a noisy and divisive government crisis that lasted the entire week I was there. The inflammatory rhetoric and the party infighting from the left and right were very ugly.

The political crisis was tied to an upcoming national election—a fierce internal power struggle that pit the far-right ultra-nationalist parties against the moderate pro-European left-of-center ruling coalition.

The Slovenian media were familiar with my in-country family relation-ships through my ex-husband. The far right tagged me a "merchant of death" and a "warmonger." Forged intelligence documents were pro-duced to discredit me as well as the US government. The Slovenian Ministry of Interior provided police protection for me everywhere I went. These incidents would become part of Slovenian political mythol-ogy called "L'Afera Kaminsky," translated to "The Kaminsky Affair."

Lockheed Martin instructed me to leave the country immediately and not have any further contact with Slovenian officials. But there was a problem. Sam was flying to Slovenia to join me after my Lockheed Martin business was done. The US ambassador, Vic Jackovich, my friend, advised me to stay in the hotel and leave with Sam immediately after his arrival.

When my jet-lagged husband arrived, I was waiting for him with my police escort in the lobby of the Holiday Inn. The ambassador had arranged for a rental car. Sam and I left Slovenia and drove over the bor-der to Trieste in Italy that same day. I left Slovenia laughing and crying at the same time.

Upon my return to the United States, the US government and Senate Majority Leader Bob Dole expressed strong displeasure and disapproval to the Slovenian government about my treatment by Slovenian authori-ties. It was bitterly ironic! I had assisted the Slovenian foreign minister, Dimitrij Rupel, and President Kučan in their efforts to raise Slovenia's profile in DC. I had helped gain official diplomatic recognition for Slovenia. In the end I had to escape from Slovenia, a small provincial country that clearly needed more time to mature politically before it could become part of the West and eventually join NATO.

In another ill-timed work visit, I arrived in the Philippines on an assignment for Lockheed Martin in the midnineties. Sam had come with me. My good friend Leticia Ramos-Shahani, sister of President Ramos, was in the Philippine Senate. She invited me to attend a Senate session to witness Filipino democracy in action. As luck would have it, we were there on the day the Philippine Senate voted overwhelmingly in favor of US withdrawal from Clark Air Force Base. I was seated in the front row as Senator Shahani's guest. On that fateful day I witnessed a major rejection of US policy that had been in effect since the early 1900s—a sad day for US-Philippine relations. In 2012 the Philippine government invited the United States to return to Clark Air Force Base once again. The Filipinos had changed their minds.

At Lockheed Martin I transitioned to working on the F-35 (Joint Strike Fighter) programs for Israel and Turkey. In 1995 I made my first trip to Turkey. I had already been to Israel many times. My work with the F-35 lasted more than fifteen years. I left Lockheed Martin in 2012. The F-35 program entailed a complex international partnership with a number of countries in Europe and Asia. I focused on Israel and Turkey, two partner countries that I knew well and that were US strategic allies. I developed strong working relationships with the Israeli Ministry of Defense, focused on the area of industrial cooperation. Some of my closest friendships with Israelis were developed during that time and have lasted over the years. Hats off to my colleagues in Israel: Amos Yadlin, Yossi Draznin, Nir Ben Moshe, Gideon Meretz, and, of course, the inimitable Yossi ben Hanan.

I analyzed the ever-changing political environment for Lockheed Martin negotiators in both countries. I identified key players and trends regarding the proposed multibillion-dollar purchase. I monitored regional press coverage about the prospective sale. It helped that I was personally acquainted with many of the Israeli and Turkish government leaders, both civilian and military.

In short, I became a frequent flyer to both countries while at the same time developing in-depth expertise on the Turkish and Israeli defense markets and their political environments. My hands-on approach to strategic planning and marketing enabled me to provide Lockheed Martin with unique insights into developments in the Middle East region. Once again, my international Rolodex served me well. Working with Bob Trice, General Jim Jamerson (ret.), and Ron Covais was very rewarding. They were my consistent and constant advocates and supporters.

In 2003 President George W. Bush appointed me to the Board of the National Defense University (NDU). I served for five years. I had previously been on the Board of the National Defense University Foundation. NDU, funded by the Department of Defense, is the premier institute of higher education for military officers. It provides Joint Professional Military Education, high-level training in the development of a national-security strategy for the US Armed Forces. I viewed the appointment as a reward for my overall service to the US military. I was now a full-fledged member of the defense establishment.

In 2005 I participated in a Capstone Mission organized by NDU and led by my friend, the capable and well-informed Admiral (ret.) Leon "Bud" Edney. Capstone is a program that allows newly selected general and flag officers to familiarize themselves with regional policy issues and military strategy related to key allied nations. I spent two weeks flying on a KC-135 refueling tanker—not the most luxurious form of transportation. The first stop was Tel Aviv. Then we proceeded to Istanbul, Naples, Rome, Bucharest, Stuttgart, and Brussels.

At each stop we were briefed by US Embassy personnel and military officers about the in-country situation. Our group included Army Rangers, Submariners, Air Force Intelligence, Green Berets, and Delta Force. A navy nurse and I were the only females. The trip was memorable in so many ways.

There were a number of very humorous incidents on this trip. I had not been told in advance that the plane had a hole in the floor for a bathroom and did not have your usual toilet paper. When we landed at Istanbul Military Airport, the stairway to leave the plane was missing. A side door of the plane was opened. The other passengers threw their luggage on the ground and jumped off the plane. Except for me. They finally found a ladder to put up to the plane so I could come down. There was applause and good-hearted laughter when I hit the ground. The entire incident was videotaped. How embarrassing! But after it was over, I was quickly enveloped in the camaraderie and teamwork of the mission, and I never gave it another thought. We moved on to the next briefing with the Turkish General Staff (TGS) and a private dinner with the deputy chief of the TGS, General Cevik Bir, that I had arranged for my traveling companions.

During the entire two weeks I spent with those guys, I felt honored and protected. They treated me like a queen. It was the adventure of a lifetime.

I had planned to participate in another Capstone Mission, this one going to Uzbekistan, Afghanistan, Pakistan, Dubai, Kuwait, and Cairo. The Bagram Air Force Base in Afghanistan was considered to be very unstable at the time, and accommodations were sketchy. I backed out of that one graciously. I found out that I would have been sleeping for three nights at the Bagram Air Base under artillery fire. At night I would have been given a flashlight to find the bathroom somewhere across the airfield. For me that was a bridge too far. Sam talked me out of it. I'm sure I would have survived the rigors, although it would have been very demanding. I still regret not having gone. I never had another chance to go on a Capstone trip. In early 2009 I was no longer on the BOV. A new president had come to town: Barack Hussein Obama.

Even though I was never able to visit Uzbekistan, I did get to know their embassy staff in DC. The Uzbek Embassy was redecorated to make it feel as if one is in the country itself. The art and furnishings are uniquely Uzbek. When President Islam Karimov came to DC for his first official visit, I was invited to the dinner at the embassy. In honor of my support for Uzbekistan diplomatic efforts in Washington, I was seated next to President Karimov. Their foreign minister also showered me with gifts. Washington had high hopes for Uzbekistan. But democracy was not in the cards for the Uzbeks. President Karimov crushed all opposition and was an authoritarian until his death in August 2016. I badly wanted to visit the magical cities of Samarkand and Bukhara on the famous medieval Silk Road. They are still on my bucket list.

In the early nineties, I was appointed to another board. AURA is the Association of Universities for Research in Astronomy. The Hubble Space Telescope was a Lockheed Martin program. AURA tracked the Hubble Space Telescope and all the other US-government-funded telescopes in Chile, Hawaii, New Mexico, and Arizona. The astronomers on the board were an interesting bunch. I, of course, was not an astronomer. I was asked to join the board because of my international contacts.

What I should have known before joining was that telescopes are usually located on remote mountaintops with difficult and sometimes treacherous access. The visits to Kitt Peak in Arizona and Sacramento Peak in New Mexico went well. The visit to Chile was another story. The drive up to the telescope location at La Serena, Chile, which is thousands of feet high, frightened me. We drove on a dirt road with no guardrails, next to long and precipitous drops to seemingly nowhere. I learned on that trip that I have a phobia of unprotected heights. By the time we arrived at our destination, I was in a state of panic and hyperventilation. Thankfully Sam had accompanied me. We exited the car. I stood shaking, hanging on to Sam on a wind-swept barren mountaintop that must look like the landscape of the moon. Everyone in our group was aware of my problem and was very sympathetic.

When we returned to the United States a few days later, I resigned from the AURA Board of Directors, after two years of service. I had learned something new about myself: I have a phobia of high places. Since I had been a skier most of my life, it was a stunning revelation for me.

Looking back on my more than twenty-five years as a consultant to the defense industry, I feel an enormous sense of gratification and achievement. I almost always worked and traveled in an all-male environment with the unquestioning support, respect, and friendship of my male colleagues. At the same time, I was able to maintain my credibility and femininity. Congressman Murtha gave me a big chance in 1989. I

earned my keep. I rose to the occasion with the help of my male cowork-
ers, who stood with me every step of the way. What an amazing journey it
was. While working on critical defense and military issues, I was serving
my country and the boots on the ground. It was an honor and a privilege. Thank you, guys! You all made it possible. I couldn't have done it
without you.

An Unlikely Duo

It was June 21, 1994. I had never traveled to Turkey. That would quickly change. I was attending a JINSA board meeting in DC. We were discussing the Israel-Turkey strategic partnership agreement that had recently taken effect.

I was seated next to a Turkish woman, Aydan Kodaloglu. Aydan had been born into a prominent and well-heeled eastern Anatolian family—the daughter of a civil engineer and a female economist. She attended an English-speaking private school founded by General Kemal Atatürk, the father of modern Turkey. She then graduated from the University of Ankara with a major in English and American literature and language. She was director of the Turkish American Association for many years, as well as the guiding light behind the Israeli-Turkish Friendship Society. Aydan is now a well-connected and respected political strategist in Ankara and Washington.

Meeting Aydan changed my life. She was energetic. She was dynamic. She was smart. We were destined to do great things together. We became soulmates, close personal friends, and professional colleagues. Our different cultures and religious backgrounds joined together to make a formidable team. It was an unusual combination. When we first met in 1994, we did not know how dramatically and quickly Turkey would become an Islamist state after the election of Prime Minister Tayyip Erdogan in 2002 and the coming to power of the AK Party.

For more than ten years, Aydan and I tried to bring the United States, Turkey, and Israel closer together. We saw ourselves as catalysts to stimulate cooperation in the region. I first visited Turkey in 1995. Thus began an extraordinary adventure that has lasted until today.

I traveled to Turkey every few months for more than fifteen years. By then I had my favorite stores, restaurants, and hotels in both Istanbul and Ankara. Aydan and I became familiar figures to most of the movers and shakers in Turkey. With her prestige and access to back me up, I regularly met with some of Turkey's top political and military leaders. We became effective interlocutors on critical issues. We spent most of our time with the secular elites, the Kemalists (Turks who had large portraits of Atatürk hanging in their homes and offices) a Turkish society that is now a fading memory.

During the 1990s the Israel-Turkey alliance was in full bloom. It was an object of pride and commitment by both countries. Aydan and I nurtured and reinforced the relationship in every way we could, through dinners, speeches, and public-relations events.

We traveled to Israel together in 2000. I arranged for Aydan to make a presentation about Turkish policy to a gathering of International Women's Forum (IWF) members representing thirty-five chapters around the world. I introduced Aydan to my Israeli friends, who then followed up with a high-level women's fact-finding mission to Turkey a year later. As a result of our efforts, the original site of the conference was moved from Tel Aviv to Jerusalem—a very symbolic statement at that time. The IWF now has a chapter in Turkey, as well as in other Muslim-majority countries, such as Egypt, Morocco, Tunisia, and Jordan. IWF reached out to Muslim women and included them in its programs and conferences. The profiles of Muslim women were then raised in their home countries, giving them status and the support to pursue women's rights issues.

In the meantime, Aydan and I became trusted confidantes as we made the rounds of posh Ottoman dinner parties in Istanbul and Ankara. We were seen as a power duo—two women who had access at the highest level and an understanding of the issues affecting the Middle East. My friendship with Aydan enabled me to learn about and understand the inner workings and social dynamics of Turkish society.

Over the years I gained the trust and confidence of my newly acquired Turkish friends. In Turkish culture, friendship is not assumed. It must be earned. Once earned, it lasts forever.

It was well-known in DC that I was knowledgeable about Turkish political and military affairs. Sadly, the political and social changes developing in Turkey after 2002 were bad and getting worse. Because of my associations in-country, I was quickly able to understand and analyze the dynamics of the new Islamist-leaning Turkey. My expertise about an important NATO country was extremely helpful for my work with the US defense industry.

General Dynamics (GD) had invested millions of dollars in an effort to produce a Turkish vehicle based on the M-1 Abrams tank. For several years I advised GD that the Turks were only interested in the tank technology, not the American tank per se. I told GD to save their money. After many years of wasted money and effort, GD finally abandoned the Turkish main battle-tank program.

Lockheed Martin Corporation and other US defense companies faced similar challenges regarding defense procurement in Turkey. In the late 1990s, Turkish military procurement policy changed. The Turkish government made the decision to develop an indigenous defense industry. They demanded technology transfer as part of any and all defense deals. Russia, Italy, and France were willing to play that game. Israel also played their game for a while. The United States was not willing to do so. It's a silly game. There are always other countries who will sell their technology to the highest bidder.

Each time I visited Ankara on business for General Dynamics or Lockheed Martin, I would stay at the Ankara Hilton. I was always given room 709, a lovely room with a view of the basketball court of the nearby Iranian Embassy—which was a little disconcerting. After several stays in room 709, I decided to ask for a different room. The hotel manager was not pleased. Apparently knowing in advance that I was coming, they had bugged room 709 for my visit. Turkish authorities were not happy about my room change. To keep them on their toes, I stayed at different hotels on future visits.

Several of the senior Turkish military leaders I met with over the years were arrested on dubious charges in 2009 by the Islamist government led by Prime Minister Erdogan. They languished in Ankara and Istanbul prisons for several years—innocent victims of a political witch hunt and a vengeful Islamist justice system. I wanted to visit them in prison to show my support but was advised against it. I felt these men were worthy US allies who deserved not to be forgotten. Eventually, several years later, they were released with all charges dropped. Their careers were ruined. They were demoralized and in poor health. Several of them died in custody for lack of adequate medical care. This unwarranted imprisonment of military leaders was a preview of things to come in Turkey.

Another Turkish-related issue was the divided island of Cyprus in the eastern Mediterranean. Often when I visited Turkey I traveled to Turkish Cyprus as well. I wanted to learn firsthand why the island continued to be the center of controversy divided between Greece and Turkey. As director of the UN office, I was the only UN official who ever dealt directly with Turkish Cyprus, much to the dismay of my superiors in New York. After I left the UN, I was invited to Turkish Cyprus as an honored guest. I had broken ranks with my fellow UN colleagues. The Turkish Cypriot leadership, especially President Rauf Denktash, greatly appreciated my courage to do so. I felt strongly that the Cyprus issue was long overdue for settlement between Greece and Turkey.

During my numerous visits to Turkey, I made time to meet with the leadership of the Turkish Jewish community. Turkey provided asylum to the Jews escaping the Inquisition in 1492. In 1927 the Jewish community numbered eighty-two thousand. In 1948 close to half of Turkey's Jews left for the newly created State of Israel. Now again Turkish Jews may soon have to make some very difficult choices. In 1995 they numbered more than thirty-five thousand. Today there are less than seventeen thousand Turkish Jews left. Many young Turkish Jews left for the United States, Israel, Canada, Australia, and elsewhere.

The situation for Jews in Turkey has changed for the worse since the 2002 election of Prime Minister Erdogan. Even though Turkish Jews are successful in business and academia, the community is now fearful and more isolated. When I met with them, I assured them they would not be forgotten should the situation deteriorate even further. Anti-Semitism is widespread among Turkey's current leadership. Turkey's Jewish community may be the only remaining diaspora community in a country with a Muslim majority. The prospects for a small minority community continuing to lead a dynamic cultural life are no longer realistic. Its long-term viability is in doubt.

During the heyday of the Israeli-Turkish alliance, the Turkish ambassador to Israel hosted a private dinner in my honor at his residence while I was in Israel. Several high-level Israeli officials attended. Ambassador Namik Tan is a close personal friend to this day. He went on to become the Turkish ambassador to the United States. He is a superb diplomat who skillfully dealt with many challenges, in both Tel Aviv and Washington. I admire him greatly.

One of those chic Istanbul dinners Aydan and I attended in Turkey was at the home of a prominent advisor to Prime Minister Erdogan. It was a lavish residence overlooking the Bosporus. Aydan and I were invited along with three other American-policy experts. Also present was Turkish Minister of the Economy Ali Babacan. During the course of our lively discussion, we asked our Turkish hosts a question: Who are your national heroes? The minister responded by naming Yāsser Arafat and Osama bin Laden. We were dumbfounded and at a loss for words. The evening ended abruptly. We all felt that, if we pushed a little harder, we probably would have heard Adolf Hitler mentioned as well. After a bit more small talk, we excused ourselves and left the table to return to our hotel in Istanbul.

That night we realized that our understanding of history was starkly different from that of our Turkish hosts. We were taken aback at what we had heard. We were Turkophiles who loved Turkey and its people and had spent many years working on their behalf. We had many Turkish friends. But we realized we were miles apart in our worldviews. The dinner that evening on the Bosporus was a turning point and an eye-opener. We realized Turkey was becoming more Islamic and less Western. A troubling finding about a supposedly friendly NATO ally.

Speaking of dinners, in DC, Aydan and I cohosted a series of highly publicized dinner events to promote US-Turkish commercial relations. We drew attention to pro-American Turkish businessmen and women who were being harassed, extorted, and treated unfairly by the Erdogan government. Power players in DC were beginning to realize that events in Turkey were spinning out of control and threatening US interests, both commercial and strategic.

The Erdogan government imposed billions of dollars in fines on businessmen and women who spoke out against the Islamization of Turkish society. Secular executives were denied government contracts and building permits. On the other hand, Islamist businesspersons who played ball with the Erdogan government were very prosperous. Aydan and I did our part to deliver this message to Washington policymakers and the media. Our Washington soirees served as a wake-up call for any and all who would listen.

September 11, 2001, changed everything. March 1, 2003, dramatically changed America's view of Turkey as a reliable and trusted ally. On that date the Turkish Parliament voted to block US troops from crossing Turkey to gain entry to Iraq from the north. On March 17, 2003, the Iraq War began without Turkish support. US military operations were seriously hampered by Turkey's decision. American lives were lost as a result. Since then most US policymakers and military strategists have viewed Turkey with suspicion and skepticism.

After the Iraq War ended, Aydan and I turned our attention to the rebuilding of the devastated country. Aydan knew some of the key players in postwar Iraq and Kurdistan, which is part of northern Iraq. We were preparing for a time when the fighting was over and the hard work of remaking Iraq would begin. We hosted the first dinner in DC to introduce a well-known Iraqi business group from Basra in southern

Iraq. The word in DC was that our dinners were not to be missed. These dinners were unique. They were a statement of unofficial government policy. It was a breakthrough!

Americans were keen to restart the Iraqi economy and lay the groundwork for American companies to get a major piece of the action. But it was not to be. The rebuilding effort was overtaken by events in 2010 when President Obama ordered all the American troops to withdraw. Today the country is divided and engaged in a bitter battle with ISIS—a brutal, radical Islamist entity. American contractors are still in Iraq, but they are operating at considerable risk. The country is engulfed by the internecine religious warfare prevalent throughout the Arab world today.

The election of President Barack Obama brought about a slight revival of the US-Turkish relationship. But it was only a temporary phenomenon. More importantly, the US military and defense establishment learned a hard lesson about the reliability and trustworthiness of their NATO ally Turkey. A lesson they will not soon forget.

In 2004 I returned to DC from a particularly troubling visit to Turkey. I prepared a report that was widely circulated in DC, in Jerusalem, and probably in Ankara as well. My report sounded the alarm about the dangerous changes taking place in Turkish society. My 2004 predictions have sadly come to pass. In retrospect I regret not circulating my message more broadly. It would take a few more years for DC policymakers to wake up and accept the reality that Turkey was now Islamist and not always a reliable ally.

My friends in the Israeli government were anxious to maintain the Israel-Turkey alliance. I shared my thinking regarding Turkey and its changing political environment with them. It was obvious to us that the Israel-Turkey relationship was going downhill fast. The Islamist Erdogan government no longer valued the alliance and was looking for an excuse—any excuse—to break it off publicly and definitively.

Prime Minister Erdogan had already publicly insulted Israeli President Shimon Peres at a Davos summit. However, it was the *Mavi*

Marmara incident in 2010 that proved to be the final nail in the coffin. The Israel Defense Forces interdicted a so-called Gaza Freedom Flotilla and inflicted nine casualties—eight Turkish nationals and one Turkish American. The incident triggered a wave of anti-Semitism and conspiracy theories in the Turkish media. Prime Minister Erdogan spoke out harshly against Israel. Ambassadors were expelled on both sides, and the partnership was over.

In my opinion, even if diplomatic relations between the two countries are restored, it will never again be as it was in the nineties. Reconciliation would be based on national interest rather than trust. As long as an Islamist government rules Turkey, full and meaningful restoration of Israel-Turkey diplomatic relations will be a pipe dream. In the Middle East, as they say, "the enemy of my enemy is my friend." In the case of Turkey, it could be said that "the enemy of my enemy is still my enemy." It remains to be seen how the latest Israel-Turkey alliance will be implemented. It will be a long and difficult road. Both the Turks and Israelis are wary and skeptical. But we shall see.

Aydan and I continue our friendship. Thankfully, she visits the United States several times a year. I have not visited Turkey since 2010. Sam and I miss the holidays we spent on yachts in the Aegean, and resorts along the Mediterranean in Bodrum and Antalya, where we laughed and drank with our Turkish friends. Aydan's fiftieth-birthday celebration in Rome with the Fendi family at our favorite Hotel Valadier near the Piazza del Popolo, and the glittering tenth-anniversary party for Aydan's consulting company at the Hotel Beluga in Bodrum, are now distant memories.

I hope someday to witness the return once again of freedom to the Turkish people. However, the dire results of recent Turkish elections are not encouraging. I will have to wait for a brighter day in the central Anatolian heartland of the modern Turkish Republic. I have promised Aydan that I will be with her in Turkey to celebrate the one hundredth anniversary of the founding of the Turkish Republic in 2023. Inshallah!

Phyllis in Monte Carlo, 1968

Phyllis with Jehan Sadat, first lady of Egypt, in Cairo, Egypt, 1980

To Phyllis Kaminsky,
With best wishes, Ronald Reagan

Phyllis with President and Mrs. Reagan and
Ambassador Jeane Kirkpatrick, circa 1984

Phyllis with National Security Advisor William Clark, circa 1984

Phyllis making a statement on behalf of the United States at the
UN Human Rights Council, Geneva, Switzerland, 2003

Phyllis with the Secretary General and the staff of the
UN Information Center, Washington, DC, 1984

Phyllis with President Milan Kučan of Slovenia and his staff, circa 1992

Signing of the Declaration of Cooperation between the
United States and Lithuania, June 26, 1998

Phyllis with cadets of the US Air Force Academy,
Colorado Springs, Colorado, 1990

Phyllis with President and Mrs. George H. W. Bush leaving Air
Force One, Andrews Air Force Base, Maryland, 1991

Phyllis Kaminsky

Phyllis with her Turkish friend and colleague Aydan Kodaloglu, 2012

Phyllis with Turkish General Staff, Ankara, Turkey, 1997

Phyllis with Israeli Prime Minister Menachem Begin, Jerusalem, Israel, 1980

Phyllis with Commander Shelly Gotman, Hatzerim
Air Force Base, Israel, circa 2008

When the Voices of Women are Heard

It's great to be a woman these days. Opportunities abound. Everything is open to possibility and promise. I have never thought of myself as a feminist. I've always thought of myself as a pioneer of sorts for women. I always believed that a woman must find her own voice. I never believed that, just because I am a woman, less is possible for me. I set my sights on making inroads into the nontraditional roles for women. In my worldview women could be leaders in the defense, space technology, electronics, and aerospace industries, as well as the national security and counterterrorism arena—the so-called man's world. We could be on the battlefield, in the war room, and at the top level of our diplomatic corps. We can play a critical role in promoting our country's national interests around the world. I was challenged by the fact that not many women were in that field. I aspired to be one of those women who could break through the barriers.

In 1989 I entered the world of the defense industry. I worked hard to gain the respect of my male colleagues in a male-dominated industry. My appointment to the Board of Visitors of the US Air Force Academy in 1989 was fortuitous. It was the right opportunity for me at the right time. It gave me access to and status with the military establishment and the defense and aerospace business. The lack of a military background did not seem to matter. It took a while, but after a few months, I became "one of the guys."

The environment for women in the most male-dominated sectors of our society is much different from and better now than it was in the early eighties. Women have worked quietly and effectively behind the scenes to bring about progress. After all men are also fathers who would like to see their daughters succeed. Women like me prove that daughters can follow in their fathers' footsteps. They now have a multitude of professional choices. They are not restricted to jobs or professions that were previously viewed as being for women only. Along the way most of my role models were my male colleagues. I learned a lot from them. In the end I spent more than twenty-five years as an international consultant to several of the giants in the defense industry.

In women's struggle to land top corporate jobs, defense contractors are now leading the change. In the past the defense industry was slow to promote women to its highest levels, in part because of its close connections to the military. Many retired officers eventually became executives at contracting firms. Some of the change came about when women who were in the military were promoted to top officer positions that were previously closed to them. These days an industry traditionally dominated by male executives looks a lot different. According to Marion Blakey, CEO of the Aerospace Industries Association, "It's a coming of age for this industry."

I have two exceptional friends who have defied the odds. Ambassador Barbara Barrett was the first woman to fly an F-14 jet fighter. Barbara also became a trained astronaut. The Honorable Mae Sue Talley was probably the first woman to head up a defense industry company, Talley Industries, more than forty years ago. These women were extraordinary trailblazers many years ago. Their careers serve as an inspiration to many women seeking to achieve and succeed in a male-dominated business environment

However, women still need to prove themselves to have an equal shot at the top. They should be credible, reliable, knowledgeable, and, last but not least, feminine. I was given that chance in 1989, and I ran with it for more than twenty-five years. Today in 2015 there is an "Old Girls' Club," as described by Jane Wells, a CNBC reporter, in November 2012.

In 2016 the CEOs of General Dynamics, Lockheed Martin, Boeing, and BAE Systems are all women.

Marillyn Hewson, CEO of Lockheed Martin, said in an April 2012 *Washington Post* interview, "I know that a lot of women look for role models in different areas so I certainly want to continue to be a role model. But I don't think it's necessarily about being a female in our business. I think it's about…my track record, my results." Carly Fiorina, former CEO of Hewlett-Packard and 2016 presidential candidate, said the same.

I was a mentor to a number of women. As a leader, I tried to inspire and prepare women in the pipeline to take up the mantle in the future. In each case I laid the groundwork for those leaders who would come after me. Giving up power is not easy. There were times when my leadership style was painful and emotional for me. Nevertheless, I continue to believe that the approach of cultivating new leadership to take over is the correct way to lead. And the beneficiaries are young women who are ready to rise.

The Jerusalem Women's Seminar was an effort on my part to highlight the potential power of high-level women to contribute to the Middle East peace process. My work with Aydan Kodaloglu in Turkey and Israel was in a similar vein. It proved that knowledgeable and committed women can become a catalyst for positive change.

In tandem with my government service, beginning in the early eighties, I touched every base I could. I served on President Reagan's Presidential Personnel Task Force on Women. I was a charter member of the International Women's Forum DC chapter. I was vice-chair of Executive Women in Government.

I also was very involved in women's issues on an international level. In the early eighties, I attended the UN's first Eleanor Roosevelt Caucus on Women. The caucus led to the founding of the International Institute for Women's Political Leadership (IIWPL). I became a director along with Madeleine Albright and Geraldine Ferraro. Members included Angela Merkel, at the time serving in the German Bundestag, and now chancellor of Germany, Ellen Johnson Sirleaf, who was in exile in the US at the time and is now president of Liberia, and Sue Clark Wood, former president of the National Party in New Zealand. Sadly, the Institute was short-lived after two initial meetings, one in Germany and the other in Costa Rica.

Geraldine Ferraro and Madeleine Albright had asked me to join the group. They knew that the institute could succeed only as a bipartisan effort. It needed a Republican woman in a leadership position. My UN title fit the bill. Sadly, both Madeleine and Gerry saw the institute as a vehicle for their personal political ambitions. I guess it was inevitable that a political institute would fail because of partisanship. Tensions developed early on. What was intended to be a powerful idea for women all over the globe died a slow, premature death.

I was also chair and founding president of the International Women's Media Foundation (IWMF). I worked closely with my cochair Gigi Geyer, a respected syndicated columnist, as well as many well-known women journalists in print and broadcasting. I'm pleased that the IWMF is now a thriving organization with an international membership and a major presence in the communications sector. You may wonder how I could have founded an organization for women journalists. I was not a working journalist. At the time I was the press officer for the National Security Council in the Reagan White House. That title gave me standing and the necessary credentials with the national press corps.

Gigi Geyer was well-known as a conservative-leaning columnist. I was a staff member of a Republican White House. Once the IWMF had garnered enough support and funding, Gigi and I were quickly replaced by two liberal-leaning women journalists. It didn't help that Gigi and I were both Republicans. We were suitably honored and recognized for our work at a gala dinner held at the Women's Art Museum in downtown DC. Gigi and I gave up our positions for what we saw as the greater good of the IWMF. It was a painful experience. Another chapter closed because of partisanship.

The IWMF is now an organization run by journalists with a particular political and social agenda. It has reinforced my view that many journalists, whether male or female, are biased and agenda driven. Many of them are lacking in professional integrity. They do not tolerate those who have a different policy view. The IWMF experience proved the point.

As a member of the US delegation, I attended the UN Conference for the UN Decade for Women, held in Vienna, Austria. As a UN official, I delivered hundreds of speeches worldwide on women's inclusion and advancement in governance and policy-making.

While at USIA I was an officer of Women in Communications, and I joined the Women's Foreign Policy Council. Speaking of breakthroughs, in 1992 while serving at USIA, I was the first woman ever to address the annual meeting of the Harry S. Truman Library Foundation. Senator Barry Goldwater and Speaker Tip O'Neill were also featured speakers.

While a director of the International Republican Institute (IRI), I chaired the first women's leadership conference post–Berlin Wall in Novgorod, Russia, in June 1993. My cochair was Frank Fahrenkopf, the chairman of the Republican National Committee. I opened the conference on June 24, 1993, as an "exciting opportunity to interact with women of the former Soviet Union as the democratic process continues to unfold in their countries." More than 150 political activists, entrepreneurs, housewives, journalists, teachers, students, and volunteers attended the conference. They came from Belarus, Estonia, Georgia, Kazakhstan, Kyrgyzstan, Latvia, Lithuania, Moldova, Russia, Turkmenistan, Ukraine, and Uzbekistan. Together we broke new ground after the fall of the Berlin Wall.

During my time in the private sector, I served as a director of several multinational companies based in London, Stockholm, Zurich, and Amsterdam. In each case I was the only woman and the only American. I enjoyed the exposure but was never entirely comfortable. On the European boards, I dealt with the ever-present "Ugly American" phenomenon once again. This time it was post 9/11, after the wars in Afghanistan and Iraq. I also felt that some anti-Semitic feelings were close to the surface. I was constantly on guard. Once again, I became a member of the old boys' club—this time in an international setting. My first board appointment was in 1997. I left boardroom service in 2015.

The corporate-board environment was demanding and invigorating. It kept me on my toes. In hindsight, it was an experience worth having.

In the early eighties, women had not yet begun to raise the issues of harassment or discrimination in the workplace. The subject was quietly accepted as part of the Washington scene. In spite of the progress women had made, women were still being penalized for taking time off to have children and care for them. They were being overlooked for promotions and salary increases. The Anita Hill episode was an eye-opener.

The case of Senator Packwood in the nineties changed the way the issue of sexual and workplace harassment was dealt with. In September of 1995, Senator Bob Packwood (R-Oregon) resigned his Senate seat after a three-year drama rather than bring further disgrace to an institution he had served for twenty-seven years. It was the Senate's first case of sexual harassment by a member that was dealt with openly and publicly.

Packwood's departure was the first major victory for women on the issue of sexual harassment. Evidence showed that the four-term senator had long made unwanted sexual advances toward ten or more women between 1969 and 1989, allegedly grabbing, fondling, and kissing female staff members and office visitors. Ironically, Packwood was an abortion-rights advocate. He championed women's causes and had the support of feminists nationwide. His actions were described as sexual harassment, but they also could have been called an abuse of power.

The Packwood story has a personal aspect for me. I had my own story to tell about Packwood. I chose to stay quiet at the time. I vividly remember the scene in his office when, after a meeting with him about an upcoming UN Conference on Women, I stood up to shake his hand and leave. The senator grabbed me and tried to kiss me. I remember yelling in shock, "Senator?" I ran out of his office trembling. I never told anyone. The shock and humiliation were too overwhelming.

Now women are no longer afraid. We are in the era of Roger Ailes and Bill Cosby. They are no longer silent. Women are learning to fight back. Some women may still choose to stay quiet. Studies indicate that the great majority of sexual harassment issues in the workplace still go unreported. However, women would find enormous support and understanding if they decided to go forward.

Looking back, I believe I helped many women realize their dreams. I can never know the full scope of the impact I have had on them. But I am confident I inspired some to make good choices, to break out and explore and excel in challenging new professional areas of opportunity. Women should be ready and willing to set an example and show others it can be done. By doing so you provide the psychological boost and incentive to others who come after you.

The female cadets at the US Air Force Academy feared retribution if they spoke up. I can only hope that they now perceive their own power and act on it.

A few pointers from my experience: Be open, accept new experiences, and seek advice. Listen to others but follow the path that is right for you. The future is limitless.

To paraphrase the Greek writer Aristophanes: When the voices of women are heard and they are the voices of clear sanity and reason, the world would do well to stop and listen.

It's great to be a woman in today's world. Everything is possible. Go for it!

A LOVE AFFAIR

Israel is a small country. Historically, small states are vulnerable and under constant threat. So it is for Israel. The country has faced three major wars since its inception in 1948. So far Israel has survived. As Golda Meir said, "Israelis have a secret weapon. We have nowhere else to go." Israel is their place—a unique blend of national identity, religion, and loyalty to the land.

Some people say that time is on Israel's side. Others believe the Bible that says, "Out of the strong came forth sweetness" (Judges 14:14). Out of a difficult situation, good will arise. Still others believe that the struggle for survival of the Jewish people will never end or will end badly. In the changing sands of the desert, where orchids never bloom, nothing is permanent. Life can change overnight.

I visited Israel for the first time in March of 1969, when I was living in Monte Carlo. Thus began a love affair that continues until today—a love affair with a tiny democracy and a nation under siege. When I returned to the United States in 1970, my love affair with Israel continued in my work for the United Jewish Appeal. It gained more strength when I married Sam in 1971. Our common love of Israel brought us closer together. Over the years our commitment to the safety and security of Israel has never changed.

My love affair continued in 1980 when I was involved with Jewish voter outreach during the Reagan-Bush campaign. It followed me into the White House in 1981 and later to the United Nations in 1983. It stayed with me during the twenty-five years I worked in the defense industry. It is an important part of who I am.

Those you love are never perfect. They make mistakes. They are easily forgiven. Israel is surrounded on all sides by hordes of medieval religious zealots. It is engaged in a fierce struggle to survive the turmoil in the Arab world. It finds itself on the frontlines of the war against religious intolerance, barbarism, and unremitting hate in a world currently blinded by fear and uncertainty. As Jeremiah said, "They have eyes and see not." Israel faces the constant threat of terrorism as well as an existential enemy in a nuclear-capable Iran.

The famed Israeli General Moshe Dayan said in 1956, "We mustn't flinch from the hatred that accompanies and fills the lives of hundreds of thousands of Arabs, who live around us and are waiting for the moment when their hands may claim our blood...That is the choice of our lives—to be willing and armed, strong and unyielding, lest the sword be knocked from our fists, and our lives severed."

The founding fathers of Israel believed that Arabs and Jews should share the benefits and the duties of statehood and that "the state will be their state as well," in the words of David Ben-Gurion. Theodor Herzl wrote about a future Jewish state where Jews and Arabs would live together in peace. Sadly, it did not come to pass, and it probably never will be as originally envisioned. I am reminded of the old proverb: "He who hates, disguises himself with his lips and harbors deceit in his heart; when he speaks graciously, believe him not."

American administrations have proven to be morally and politically unable to effectively deal with the phenomenon of radical political Islam. We should take the words of Islamic radicals seriously. The radical Muslims mean what they say. In my view, when the Arab world is convinced that the Jewish State of Israel is indestructible and permanent, then there will be peace, and coexistence will have a chance.

The horror of the Holocaust seventy years ago did not change the world, nor did it change human nature. Europeans view Israel as a reminder of their crimes of colonialism and the Holocaust. Innocent civilians are being killed in Israel and elsewhere around the world. Once again the world is silent. Anti-Semitism is back in fashion again. People *do* forget.

In 1923 my father's mentor, Vladimir Jabotinsky, had the foresight to sound the alarm that the Arabs would not welcome the Zionist enterprise with open arms. He predicted that the Jews would have to be stronger and prevail by force of arms if necessary. He was the one who rekindled the idea of a Jewish army as the first step to Jewish nationhood. He favored the concept of military preparation but always hoped that it would not be necessary. This is the same Jabotinsky who ran from one synagogue to another in the shtetls of eastern Europe. He warned them about the growing strength of Hitler in Germany and begged them to leave. He saw the situation as a matter of life and death. Some people listened and left. My father was one of them. Many stayed.

Jabotinsky was likened by many to Winston Churchill, who raised a similar alarm about Hitler with the British people. Tragically, my father's mentor was vindicated by subsequent events in Europe—World War II and the Holocaust—and millions died. Winston Churchill also said, "Some people like the Jews and some do not. But no thoughtful man can deny the fact that they are, beyond any question, the most formidable and most remarkable race which has appeared in the world."

At the end of World War II, the world learned about the Jews' struggle to survive in the concentration camps and ghettos—their valiant attempts to fight back and defend themselves against the Nazis. Today resistance to tyranny is the mantra of the Jewish state. Some historians believe that six million Jews were killed because they did not have an army, they did not have a state, they did not have political protection. They were rendered defenseless and unarmed. Never again.

Seventy years later, the Jewish people can defend themselves by themselves.

The world marveled at the determination of the tattered remnants of Jews who emerged from the Holocaust, the death camps, the internment camps, and the dangerous voyage by sea to reach the land of Israel.

The world witnessed hundreds of thousands of Jews forced to leave Iraq, Syria, Yemen, Iran, Egypt, Lebanon, and Ethiopia—former rabbis, students, teachers, farmers, and street peddlers. They were black, white, brown—all colors. They left everything behind.

Lo and behold, the world was stunned to see this determined group of survivors build the land of Israel. These courageous souls became the nucleus of a mighty defensive military machine, the Israel Defense Forces (IDF), one of the fiercest fighting forces in the world, a strong, sophisticated, united army fielded by a vibrant democracy and a global technology leader. After the Holocaust, the Jewish people who survived would have preferred to be left alone to build a country and make their tiny strip of desert bloom to recreate the biblical land of milk and honey. But that was only a dream.

Israel has been in an almost perpetual state of conflict of some kind since its founding in 1948. Against great odds, the IDF won the Arab wars launched against it from the first day of its existence on May 14, 1948: the War of Independence, the Six-Day War in June of 1967, and the Yom Kippur War in October of 1973. At first the world supported IDF victories. Then demographics changed. Postcolonial Europe and newly independent Arab nations rose up against Israel. The world was confronted with a new phenomenon: the Jewish warrior. Israel was deemed to be wrong because it was strong. Jews were no longer a symbol of powerlessness—the perpetual scapegoat for whatever went wrong. Surprise! Jews were no longer the underdog, no longer the victim. The Jews were fighting back. And they were winning.

In a memorable moment for me in June 1982, then Prime Minister Menachem Begin on a visit to Washington responded to a statement from then Senator Joe Biden on the Senate Foreign Relations Committee that threatened an aid cutoff. He said, "Don't threaten us with cutting off your aid. It will not work. I am not a Jew with trembling knees. I am a proud Jew with 3,700 years of civilized history. Nobody came to our aid when we were striving to create our country. We paid for it. We fought for it. We died for it. We will stand by our principles.

We will defend them. And, when necessary, we will die for them again, with or without your aid," and he added, "We do not want a single soldier of yours to die for us." That statement moved me, and it has left its mark on my thinking.

My love affair dates back to my immigrant childhood and my parents' struggle to make a new life for their family. I have vivid memories of the stories my father told me about World War II. I heard my parents talk to one another in hushed Yiddish. I was young, but I understood the sadness and the tears. I knew the news was bad. People were dying. Every day they received letters or bad news about friends and relatives. Some had survived. Many others had not. My father's dedication to the idea of a homeland for the Jewish people was his dream—a dream he lived his life by. My love affair is my way of honoring him and his life.

I, too, have a personal stake in the land of Israel. So I satisfy myself with frequent visits. We recently visited my cousin Phyllis Avivi and her wonderful children and their families in 2016. Phyllis and I lived together in Montreal when we were young. My Israeli Rolodex bulges with names of friends and colleagues I have known and worked with over the years. I content myself by knowing I made a small difference in the critical struggle for Israel's survival. I worked behind the scenes, quietly and lovingly. I was part of an effort to keep Israel strong and well equipped for present and future threats.

Over the years Israel's defense equipment had become outdated, worn out, and less effective. Israel required new, modern, and advanced defense products to counter the growing threats in the region. My work at Lockheed Martin with the F-16 and the Joint Strike Fighter—the F-35 an even more advanced jet fighter—contributed to Israel's security.

In the face of daily threats, Israel continues to send a different message to the world. Israelis are about life, creativity, technology breakthroughs, clean water, education, agricultural technology, advances in medicine, and health care in an environment of freedom and prosperity. Israel is a miracle in the desert! Israel's response to the daily threats is to be one of the freest and happiest countries in the world.

Surprisingly in the face of external challenges, social cohesion in Israel is now greater than ever. Israelis accept the fact that this is where they are destined to live and die. They are determined to live joyfully even though peace is not breaking out anytime soon. The majority are proud to be Israelis, and most Israelis are satisfied with their lives. They describe Israel as a good place to live, knowing that they will have to live by the sword for a long time to come. David's slingshot has become David's Sling, a powerful missile system recently successfully tested.

I have always believed that if Israel's survival is threatened and the country remains insecure, then Jews will not be secure anywhere in the world, including in the United States. Right now it is particularly threatening for Jewish students and professors who are pro-Israel on American campuses. Some Jews under stress try to become less Jewish. They strive only to be normal and accepted. They have not yet absorbed the reality that every Jew is viewed as an Israeli by the non-Jewish world.

The basic goal of Israel's enemies is the destruction of the Jewish state. You ask, how could this conflict end if your enemies want to annihilate you, your religion, and your country? The Muslim world must accept the fact that the Jewish people are home—no longer wandering over the face of the globe—and they are not leaving their small plot of land. As Prime Minister Netanyahu recently said at the fortieth-anniversary commemoration of the Entebbe hostage rescue in Kenya, Israel has proved to the world that "Jews were powerless no more" and that "good can triumph over evil."

At this time peace and cooperation in the region seem distant. They will only come when the Arab world accepts the fact and reality of Israel's existence and the biblical connection of the land to the Jewish people. My love affair with the land of Israel endures. It is here to stay, as is the land of Israel.

LIKE FATHER LIKE SON

I was fortunate to be the mother of two exceptional sons. They have given me so many reasons to be proud of them. David is an architect like his father. Glenn is a lawyer like his father.

Glenn was a curly-haired child who loved life and had lots of friends. Early on he had trouble pronouncing his last name. He called himself Glenn Minsky. He was very much a part of my life during the Reagan years. Like David before him, Glenn followed me in my career. He shared the entire Washington experience with me during the eighties— easily the best years of my life. He somehow managed to remain normal, nonpartisan, and clearheaded as we lived through the political shenanigans that took place in our nation's capital.

Glenn was at breakfast every morning eating his Fruit Loops and cheering me on. He was my frequent escort to White House events, visiting ambassadors abroad and attending Fourth of July picnics on the White House lawn. He did well in school and was not too impressed with the pomp and circumstance surrounding my glamorous job. During summer breaks he had a taste of the political game. He interned in Congressman Jack Murtha's office and at America-Israel Public Affairs (AIPAC) headquarters in DC.

Glenn attended Pomona College in Claremont, California, in 1992. Sam and I flew out to California to hand-deliver our youngest child to the school. I'll admit it was very hard for me. Glenn and I were very close. When the time came, Glenn chose a college far away from DC. It was time for him to strike out on his own. He chose well. Pomona was the perfect academic setting and an excellent personal experience for him.

His college dorm room was very small. Glenn was five feet ten inches. His roommate, Jamie Bernald, was six feet seven inches. Jamie's parents had brought him to school accompanied by his special extra-long mattress. I can still see us dragging the extra-long mattress up the steps into a room that barely held two people. Jamie and Glenn became lifelong friends. We still laugh about the dorm scene so many years later.

Leaving Glenn at Pomona was very emotional for me. Glenn may not have realized that he was my anchor in reality in DC, as David had been when I was living in Monte Carlo. However, we settled Glenn into his dorm and said a teary good-bye to our baby. It was the beginning of a new chapter for us. Sam and I were now empty nesters.

After graduation from Pomona, Glenn went on to a year abroad at Hebrew University in Jerusalem. Because of my professional involvement with Israel and Turkey, Glenn visited both countries several times in order to see and learn for himself.

Following in his dad's footsteps, he then attended law school at the University of Michigan. After graduation he spent a year at a hotshot Washington law firm. It was not a good experience. It was too cutthroat. Glenn did not have the required killer instinct. He wanted to enjoy life. Instead, he chose a legal career with the US government, first at the Department of Commerce and now at the Department of Homeland Security with a specialty in export compliance and technology transfer issues. Glenn works in DC, the town he knows best, where he has many friends and good memories. I like to think that my time in the White House and our life together in DC contributed to his decision to work for the government and serve our country.

Glenn has grown to be a caring, honest, and smart young man. He is a born leader with a large stable of friends and acquaintances all over the world. In many ways his interpersonal skills and love of family have kept us all on the same page.

In August 2013 Glenn married Toby Bulloff, a trademark attorney, in a traditional Jewish wedding ceremony and celebration at the Western Reserve Historical Society in Cleveland, Ohio, Toby's hometown. The wedding hall was filled with family and friends representing every aspect of their lives from grade school through law school. It was a long-awaited event for our family. Glenn was thirty-nine when he finally gave up bachelorhood. He waited a very long time to find the right woman. He met Toby at a DC bar while watching a Michigan football game. Toby and her parents were University of Michigan alumni. Sam and I were as well. The wedding celebration was a Wolverine victory in every sense of the word.

The best was yet to come. On October 20, 2015, Bella Sydney Kaminsky was born at Sibley Hospital in DC. From the moment Bella was born, she was beautiful, healthy, and pink. Sam and I were at the hospital for the happy event. It was a long wait for this great gift of life. She is a true blessing!

Even though there was a thirteen-year spread between David and Glenn, it didn't seem to matter much. They got along well and were always going through different stages of growing up. David loved life in a small town—Johnstown, Pennsylvania. He has kept up his Johnstown friendships all these years. When the time came, he did not let any grass grow under his feet. He went off to college at Princeton and Harvard. He was following in his father's footsteps as a Princeton student and a visionary architect.

He experienced the same rite of passage as Glenn. He also interned in the office of Congressman Jack Murtha. David had a front-row seat to observe DC politics in deadly action. He served during the summer of the congressional scandal known as Abscam. Congressman Murtha had some involvement in the Abscam scandal but was later cleared of all charges after a congressional investigation. But Murtha's image was damaged, and he was personally deeply scarred by the incident.

David settled in Boston after graduation from Harvard Graduate School of Design and became one of its leading architects. Boston was an excellent choice for him. It is a booming metropolis with top colleges and universities and many young people who decide to stay on after graduation from one of the area schools. David is comfortable and accepted in Boston. His gay lifestyle is welcomed. He has become a young and creative leader of a liberal and diverse society. He climbed the ladder quickly based on his extraordinary talent for design and urban planning. His architectural structures and urban designs are now well-known in the United States and abroad. His excellent people skills contributed to his amazing success.

Boston society can be closed to newcomers who are not Boston "Brahmins." However, the city rewards those who are committed to the worlds of arts and culture. David served as chairman of the Boston Council for the Arts for several years. At the age of forty-nine, he was the youngest architect to be nominated and accepted as a fellow by the American Institute of Architects.

I am so proud of the man David has become. He has received so many awards for architecture and urban leadership that I have lost count. He was voted New England Man of the Year several years ago, and he has garnered on the average an award a month for the last few years. In 2015 he was named by *Boston Magazine* as the top urban architect in the Boston area. His architectural firm, Hacin and Associates, is a hotshot twenty-six-person boutique design firm with a global client list. In short, he is a successful, respected, talented architect-designer in one of America's major cities. For David, the sky is the limit. Throughout his life and brilliant career, he has remained as devoted and loving to me as he was during his early years.

David's partner, Tim Grafft, is the deputy director of the Massachusetts Film Commission. On October 12, 2014, after a twenty-seven-year relationship, David and Tim were married in a brilliant and moving event held at the Benjamin Franklin Institute in Boston. The gay Jewish-Irish wedding was and still is the talk of the town. The wedding was a testimony of love! Easily the most beautiful and meaningful celebration of life that anyone has ever attended.

David and Tim had a beloved schnauzer dog named Oscar who died in December 2015 at the age of fourteen. David wrote Oscar's obituary, which I share with you. The obituary tells you a lot about David and the kind of person he is.

Oscar was born in Sterling, Massachusetts on May 7, 2002 and came to us in the months after 911. As most of us recall, the whole country felt unsure about the future and we were all looking for a sense of security and comfort, mostly at home. I had waited a very long time for a dog since growing up with my own schnauzer, Spritzer, who died suddenly the week after I left for college.

Oscar was my sidekick. He was almost always with me as our office grew, barking at delivery people and racing around the conference room in his winter booties, defusing tension and delighting visitors. Oscar was famous in his own way. He appeared in Interior Design magazine, Boston magazine, and on the front page of the Boston Globe in the masthead. He was the Chief Marketing Officer of Hacin and Associates. His silhouette graces the entrance to the small dog run in our Boston neighborhood that Oscar inspired and I designed. Oscar taught us much about life—life is fleeting and we are so often not paying attention. 14 years—gone just like that—another chapter ends. It was a very happy one. Thanks Oscar. You will be missed.

Ralph Waldo Emerson said that "men are what their mothers made them." I was determined to set a positive example for my children. I feel that I have done so. Just as in many other families, my sons see the world differently than I do. It is a reflection of their generation and the changing times that are part of the social and political dynamics of the twenty-first century. We respect each other's opinions, and we follow the path of "to each his own."

David and Glenn are my greatest inspiration—my enduring legacy. Their love for me made it all possible.

HERE COMES THE SUN

September 11, 2001, changed everything for me and for almost everyone I know. Each one of us lost something that day. We lost our feeling of security and our optimism about the future. Our loss was replaced by serious concern for our children and grandchildren, coupled with the fear that America would be a constant target of terrorists in the world for many years to come. We had one overriding question: Would our country be prepared to deal with those threats?

Shortly after 9/11, Sam decided to fully retire. My career was slowing down as well. There were signs that Lockheed Martin Corporation, my principal client, was reorganizing. My colleagues whom I had worked with for twenty-five years were leaving or retiring. The management of the companies on whose corporate boards I served for many years suddenly realized I was over seventy years old, the normal age for retirement. It was time for new blood. They were right.

Our children and grandchildren are scattered all across the country, in Boston, Bethesda, Denver, LA, San Diego, Las Vegas, Phoenix, and Tucson. Sam and I decided to move to the growing Southwest. We decided upon Scottsdale, Arizona. It was an easy decision. I always loved the desert because it reminds me of Israel. The colorful desert flowers and the stark mountain scenery, not to mention the weather and relaxed lifestyle, have brought us immeasurable joy, contentment, and many wonderful new friends. Scottsdale has turned out to be an excellent choice for us. We are doing what we like to do and spending time with people we want to be with.

In 2003 we bought our first home in North Scottsdale, at Legend Trail on a beautiful golf course embedded with giant, dramatic boulders. The Phoenix metro area is spread out and in rapid development. We realized very quickly that distances between places were greater than we had anticipated. In 2008 we moved closer to downtown Scottsdale, to a Santa Barbara–style home abutting the Pima-Salt River Indian Reservation. From our window we see miles and miles of cacti, wild horses, and raw desert. The Arizona sunsets are daily happenings of incomparable beauty. For me the Valley of the Sun is paradise.

Sam and I were ready for the change. Over the years my life in Washington had become too intense and emotionally draining. The political environment had changed. I needed to "smell the roses" and "disengage," as my children often said. Of course, that was easier said than done. The Roman Emperor Marcus Aurelius said, "Your days are numbered. Use them to throw open the windows of your soul to the sun." And so I did.

We kept our condo in Chevy Chase, Maryland, while I continued to juggle my remaining career commitments. I traveled back and forth to DC and overseas. In July 2015 I received a phone call from the president of Kaba Mas Ltd., the US subsidiary of Kaba Corporation in Zurich, Switzerland. Kaba Mas was the last board position I retained. The president advised me that my term of service as a director had come to an end. Strangely enough, I was not sad or troubled, nor was I surprised. I'd had a good run with Kaba since 1994. There were still many things left to do. I was anxious to play the piano once again after so many years. I decided to write this autobiography for my children, grandchildren, and great-grandchildren. I was content. I was healthy. My passion was undiminished. I was not leaving. I was just stepping back. I could still make a difference.

In 1992 Sam and I spent a week in Incline Village, Nevada, exploring northern California. We had just dropped Glenn off in Claremont, where he would begin his college years at Pomona College. We were feeling a bit sad. We decided to get to know northern California a little better. We needed time to digest our whole new lifestyle without Glenn. We rented a car and started driving. We ended up in Incline Village. The time we spent there was perfect in every way. Lake Tahoe is spectacular; the weather was perfect; the sky was almost always blue. And we felt closer to Glenn in Pomona. We bought a small townhouse in Incline Village. We called it our West Coast base. Both David and Glenn were avid skiers. Alpine, Squaw Valley, and Northstar were our favorite slopes. I loved the mountains and was a pretty good skier. We shared many happy times en famille in Lake Tahoe, one of the most beautiful locations in North America. Over the years the kids and grandkids came up for vacations. There were memorable family reunions, Thanksgiving celebrations, and ski holidays for all of us. Sam and I ended our skiing careers a few years ago when snowboarding was introduced to the slopes. We realized we might fall and get hurt or slammed by a snowboarder. We never thought of that possibility when we were younger. We became more cautious as the years went by. Our family cherishes the memories of that beautiful place in the woods close to the lake; it was ours for fourteen years.

Sam and I returned to Lake Tahoe for a brief vacation in 2015. We visited our old haunts and favorite restaurants. Everything was still there. Nothing much had changed. It was as if time had stood still since 2006 when we sold it. We will return again. For us Tahoe will always be a very special place.

Our new life in Scottsdale was rudely interrupted one day in late August 2006. I received a call from my doctor in Maryland advising me that my recent mammogram showed an early-stage cancerous growth in my right breast. Immediately, all our plans were put on hold. On October 6, 2006, less than five weeks after the diagnosis, I underwent a lumpectomy. I was one of the lucky ones. The cancer was noninvasive. It was early stage. It had not spread. After six weeks of radiation ended on December 9, 2006, Sam and I flew back to Scottsdale to start our new life all over again.

Almost at the same time my breast cancer was diagnosed in 2006, Sam and I reluctantly decided it was time to sell the place in Tahoe. It was a wrenching decision for all of us. At one point we had four residences: Johnstown, Pennsylvania; Potomac, Maryland; Incline Village, Nevada; and Scottsdale, Arizona. It was time to lighten up a bit. We sold our original home in Johnstown in 2002.

Ironically the closing for the sale of the house in Incline Village was on October 6, 2006, the same day as my breast-cancer surgery. Sam flew out to Lake Tahoe the weekend prior to surgery to close out our place. David flew in from Boston to be with me for the weekend prior to surgery. That weekend I spent with my two boys was a very special time for me. I was truly happy in spite of the ordeal I was facing. The three of us spent quality time together, laughing and loving. My boys gave me the strength to confront the surgery. Their love and support made it so much easier.

Speaking of love, Glenn delivered me to the hospital on Monday morning, October 6, 2006, at eight o'clock. I told him to go to the office and put in a day's work at the Department of Homeland Security since I probably would not be done until late afternoon. I called Glenn at noon to tell him that everything was going well and that the surgery would begin shortly.

I'll never forget his next words to me: "Mom, I'm in the parking lot of the hospital. I couldn't go to the office. I'm waiting for you here until they call me to pick you up. I love you." And at four that afternoon, Glenn drove me home from the hospital.

Sam surprised me by flying in from Tahoe after the house closing, arriving in time to be at the house in Maryland for my homecoming from the hospital. Those are the moments that stay with you forever. Those are the times when you realize how much you are loved. Those are the times that bring quick tears. Those are the precious moments of life.

I often have tried to visualize what it must have been like for my mother and father when they arrived in the port of Halifax on a cold, gray day in January 1930. In 2010 Sam and I took a cruise leaving from New York and sailing through the Saint Lawrence Seaway to visit Canada, with a stopover in the port of Halifax. When we disembarked, we wandered around the harbor and found the Canadian Museum of Immigration. A very interesting find! The museum had data about immigrant debarkations at Halifax as far back as 1875. I knew that my parents had come in January 1930. It was relatively easy to find the ship manifest for the *Lituania*. And there it was…My mother's name was handwritten at the end of the ship manifest because she was a last-minute add-on to the passenger list. I dissolved in tears at the sight of her name. I can only imagine how difficult it must have been to cross the Atlantic in ten days in the heart of winter, alone and with no belongings in steerage. My parents' story was there in black and white. My mother identified herself as a student. My father as a teacher. My mother went to live with her older brother, Jack, in Montreal. My father joined his older sister, Edith, also in Montreal. My mother had six dollars in her pocket. My father had fifteen dollars. We photocopied all the details from the ship manifest for David and Glenn. A little wiser and sadder, Sam and I reboarded our cruise ship with so many of my questions finally having answers.

Five years ago a good friend, David Siegel, was appointed consul general of the State of Israel for the western United States, based in Los Angeles. Phoenix was part of his area of responsibility, and he visited Arizona frequently. The strategic partnership between Arizona State University (ASU) and Ben-Gurion University in Beersheba, Israel, was a labor of love for three years. I worked closely with David and his staff behind the scenes to bring this project to fruition. Finally, in 2015, Dr. Michael Crow, president of ASU, hosted an official dinner to announce the signing of the agreement between the two universities. It was a brilliant and groundbreaking affair. I was proud to be a small part of it. Another chapter in my love affair with the land of Israel.

During my time working on the ASU project, I mentored a young man, Josh Hoyt, who was president of the ASU Student Council in his senior year. A young man like Josh represents our country's future. He was a dedicated student, an ambitious and gregarious young man who will do great things. He graduated at the top of his class and was on his way to law school. In the interim he decided to deal with growing anti-Israel sentiments on a number of college campuses. He joined the staff of the Israeli Consulate in Los Angeles as director of Academic Affairs and as director of Interfaith Affairs, and he served for three years. He is currently vice-president of the Ulmer Institute, founded by Bishop Kenneth Ulmer in Los Angeles. Josh is now doing groundbreaking rehabilitation work in minority communities for wounded and struggling veterans, making use of specialized Israeli technology. I am convinced that Josh will play a major role in the political arena in the years to come.

I am also working with Regional Director Lisa Hartsock to establish a Reagan Foundation presence in Arizona. Ronald Reagan spent many years living in Phoenix near the famed Biltmore Hotel and was personally known to many Phoenix residents. We are building support and funding for the Ronald Reagan Leadership Institute to be built in DC. This effort means a lot to me. It brings back memories of the best years of my life, the extraordinary moment in history when I was part of a revolution—the Reagan Revolution. Arizona is Reagan country. Another good reason for me to be in Arizona.

When I first arrived in Arizona, I was reintroduced to a woman whom I greatly admired during my time in the Reagan administration. Mae Sue Talley is one of the most prominent and well-known personalities in the Phoenix area. I remember Mae Sue as the ambassador to the Caribbean Basin initiative, as an advisor to NASA, and as a member of DACOWITS (Defense Advisory Committee for Women in the Services), among her many other appointments in the Reagan administration.

Mae Sue was a personal friend of Nancy and Ronald Reagan, going back to the days before Ronald Reagan became governor of California. We see each other often to reminisce and catch up. Mae Sue is in her midnineties. She has a wonderful memory filled with personal stories of the Reagans. It is a joy and a treat to be able to spend time with her and relive the glorious days of the Reagan Revolution.

In 2012 the Phoenix FBI Field Office selected me to participate in the FBI Citizens Academy—a six-week course of briefings on counterterrorism, drug and sex trafficking, white-collar crime, and border immigration issues. It was an amazing and worthwhile experience bringing together citizens from the various ethnic communities in the Phoenix metro area to serve as the local eyes and ears of the FBI.

The meetings were held at FBI headquarters in Glendale, Arizona. I arrived late for the first class because I missed my exit off the parkway. I sat down in the first empty seat I saw. The older gentleman seated next to me turned to introduce himself to me and said, "Hi. I'm Mohammed. Glad to meet you." For a second I thought I was in the wrong meeting room. But I was very wrong. Mohammed turned out to be the former minister of agriculture in Somalia before the disintegration of the country. He was now representing the over thirty thousand Somalis who have settled in Arizona. Mohammed and I became friends, and I continue to see him at FBI alumni functions from time to time. Each person who was part of my class was dedicated and committed to doing his or her part. I was honored to be selected for the academy. I received a certificate of graduation at a gala closing dinner held at the Paradise Valley Country Club.

Soon after our arrival in Arizona, I joined the Phoenix Committee on Foreign Relations and various other civic organizations. Scottsdale, being a retirement community, has a large number of so-called discussion groups that tackle the issues of the day as well as controversial political issues from time to time.

One of the premier discussion groups in Scottsdale is called "The Wiseguise." It was started by a well-known Scottsdale doctor, Dr. Merv Lakin, who has since passed away. Since his death, a group of members has been carrying on with the Friday lunch speaker programs. Wiseguise was originally for men only—former CEOs, retired military and intelligence professionals, retired bankers, doctors, and professors. A few months after my arrival in Scottsdale, Dr. Lakin asked me to join. By doing so I hoped to open future invitation possibilities for women. There are now several women who participate regularly.

I tried to leave politics behind and disengage as my children asked me to do. It was difficult to do that. It's in my blood and my handshake.

Sam and I hosted several election-night parties over the years. However, the last few elections were so nerve-racking for all our friends that we gave that up. Now we prefer to watch the returns with a few like-minded friends in a quieter setting.

Sam and I host an annual Valentine's Day Sweethearts dinner at the Ancala Country Club. The Kaminsky Salon, as it has come to be known, has become an annual event for seven to eight couples who look forward to speaking their mind on the issues of the day—at least once a year.

Cruising is always on the agenda. In 2008 we were invited to join four couples from Minnesota and a retired rear admiral and her husband on a Celebrity cruise to the Baltic States and Northern Europe, including Russia and Scandinavia, including Finland. Our close friend, Barbara Barrett, was serving as the US ambassador in Helsinki. Barbara and her staff gave us royal treatment on our short stopover, and we were able to witness the presentation of her credentials to the Finnish president. A three-day visit to Saint Petersburg was extremely enlightening. The best parts of the cruise were our dinner discussions and the blending of our very different backgrounds. The cruise produced lifelong friendships. We try to meet once a year for a cruise reunion get-together.

In a blast from the past, in 2014, fifty-five years after I left Geneva, Switzerland, Sam and I were vacationing in Maine. We had lunch in Camden with John D. Macomber, my former boss at McKinsey International in Geneva. We were reunited by a good friend in Maine who had attended school with John. John and I reminisced, recollected, and reunited. We shared our memories of that fateful day, November 22, 1963, when President Kennedy was taken from us. I gave him a summary of what I had been up to since I left Geneva so many years ago.

In early 2016, my sister, Sharon, passed away peacefully and gracefully in her sleep. Sharon had not been well for many years. I will always remember when my mother and I crossed the border by train from Canada to the United States in September 1945. Sharon was nine months old, and the train conductor remarked that she had the most beautiful blue eyes he had ever seen.

Sharon was a pioneer for women in her own right as the first Jewish stewardess hired by Pan American Airways. She was so proud and beautiful in her Pan Am uniform. She visited me in Monte Carlo on the weekend the United States landed on the moon for the first time. Many people said she looked like Loretta Young, the actress.

Sadly, the last few years of her life were lonely and challenging health-wise. Happily, Sharon was visited by her daughter, Jennifer, and her two grandchildren, Levi and Maya, on Thanksgiving of 2015. Jennifer lives in Melbourne, Australia, with her husband, Chris Maxwell. She is my only niece and is very special to me. Melbourne is a bit far for frequent visits, but we stay in regular touch. My son David and his partner, Tim, were with Sharon the last weekend of her life. My sister was a very compassionate woman who loved animals and cared deeply about people who were suffering hunger and repression. She never wanted to be old. Now she never will be. She is finally at peace with herself and the world.

I feel fine about retirement. It's a time to think, to read, and to write. It's a time to enjoy children, grandchildren, and great-grandchildren and to be with friends. It's a time to enjoy, to appreciate, and to reflect. Most of all it's a time to love and be loved.

As the Beatles said many years ago, "Here comes the sun, Here comes the sun, and I say, It's all right."

REFLECTIONS

Yesterday when I was young, the taste of life was sweet
as rain upon my tongue. And only now I see how the
years ran away. Yesterday when I was young.

—JULIO IGLESIAS

Looking back on my life, I realize my plate was always full. The demands of my career were ever present. The commuter marriage Sam and I lived for twenty-three years was not always as easy and wonderful as it may sound. Living together again 24-7 in 2005 was a new experience. We had to get to know one another all over again. At any given moment, there was a child or grandchild who needed advice, money, encouragement, or a little extra loving. Very often they needed help with a college application, a résumé, or a job interview. My mother always told me that "you can't dance at every wedding." Nevertheless, I was determined to do just that. Keeping up with the Kaminskys is almost a full-time job.

The daunting challenge of being a successful stepmother and step-grandmother was a critical part of the last forty-five years of my life, beginning in 1971 when I married Sam. Sam's divorce was a difficult one. His children were deeply affected by the breakup. I was determined to do the right thing for Sam and his children, especially after their mother passed away in 1986. In addition to my sons, David and Glenn, there were four children, Sherry, Louis, Jay, and Philip, and eventually nine grandchildren, Ashley, Cara, Hannah, Haley, Jamie, Josh, Justin, Morgan, and Bella, and one great-grandchild, Carter. I made the extra effort to love and care for them as if they were my own. Being a stepparent is much more complicated than being a parent. A stepparent must make a conscious choice to love and be part of someone's life. I made that choice willingly. Now my most gratifying moments come when the kids call me Mom or Grandma. They are an important part of my life and always will be. They are a part of my love for Sam, my husband of forty-five years.

More recently Glenn and Toby have given us Bella, a beautiful granddaughter who has brought me unending joy and literally changed my life. Bella is named after my mother and carries my Hebrew name, Tzipporah. In the space of two years, both of my sons were married, and I became a first-time grandmother. Jamie, another granddaughter, has just announced her engagement to Jesse, her long-time beau. There will be many weddings and great-grandchildren in the years to come. My cup runneth over.

My parents believed America to be a country of possibility—the possibility of making things happen, of turning possibility into opportunity, and of having the freedom to determine your own destiny. "I am proud to be an American where at least I know I'm free"—the inspiring words of Lee Greenwood's famous song, which I highlighted in the commencement address I delivered to Utica College in May of 1991, express my parents' feelings about America.

In 2016 Americans find themselves living in a topsy-turvy world—a world filled with anarchy, chaos, and violence. I am apprehensive and fearful for the ones I love. I never experienced this feeling before. I was lucky growing up in the fifties and sixties, sometimes referred to as America's "age of innocence." Life was so much simpler and so much more honest. We were proud to be Americans. We responded quickly and positively to President Kennedy's call to "ask not what your country can do for you, ask what you can do for your country." Fear of the "other," uncertainty about the future, and daily anxiety were not part of our lives. We felt protected and safe. We were not divided against one another. We actually spoke to one another instead of sending e-mails or instant messages. I yearn for those days again, as in "The Way We Were," sung by Barbra Streisand. If you didn't grow up in the fifties, you may have missed the greatest time in America's history.

I'm a worrier. I worry about voter apathy and ignorance, the harsh rhetoric, the confusion about our past and present role in the world, the lack of civility and honesty in our national debate, and the dumbing down of our culture. Americans are dealing with economic uncertainty, job insecurity, wage stagnation, mounting debt, the growing burden of entitlements, and the giddying global volatility. I worry about America and Americans in the digital age of ISIS. I worry a lot about what lies ahead for my children and grandchildren.

But I'm an optimist when it comes to America. Americans are resilient. I am hopeful that we will recapture our unity and strength as a nation and that the beacon of light and freedom will be rekindled. "We shall overcome," to echo the words of Martin Luther King so many years ago. And be proud of our "shining city on the hill," in the words of President Reagan.

Even though my parents and most of their family escaped the Holocaust, Jewish people of my generation are still haunted by the tragedy. The Holocaust is still fresh in my mind, and it colors my thinking. It subconsciously defines how I view the world. The golden land that held out the dream of freedom is changing for Americans and for American Jews as well. Perhaps I am more sensitive and attuned to these changes than others because of my immigrant background.

More and more it seems like the Western world has only taken a short vacation from history. College campuses are awash in anti-Semitism. Affinity with the Judeo-Christian way of life is being diluted and minimized. The dual-loyalty question for Jews is ever present. The old hatreds and buried prejudices have returned. We are living in a post-post-Holocaust era, and once again the world order is disintegrating.

The struggle of good versus evil has resumed. History has proven that Jews do not benefit from a fractured body politic.

The communications industry also troubles me. It has become too powerful and agenda driven. Accurate news reporting happens just by chance. Through its politically biased reporting and negative and inaccurate depiction of Israel and its leaders, the media plays an all-important role in influencing the opinions of the American people and contributes to a rise of anti-Semitism worldwide. This is very disturbing!

I strongly believe that we ignore history at our peril. I closed almost every speech I made over the years with three quotes, including one from George Santayana: "Those who do not remember history are condemned to repeat it." And another from the ancient Greek historian Thucydides: "The present, while never repeating the past exactly, must inevitably resemble it." And still another from Lord Halifax: "The best way to suppose what may come is to remember what is past." These three well-known quotes have special resonance for the Jewish people.

I've worked with Princess Grace of Monaco; Mayor John Lindsay; Presidents Ronald Reagan, George H. W. Bush, and George W. Bush; Secretary-General Pérez de Cuéllar; Ambassador Jeane Kirkpatrick; a number of high-level military officers; and many others of note too numerous to mention. It's been an exciting ride, which I've shared with you.

I've reached the time in my life when reflection sets in. It's sort of like writing your own eulogy. I have concluded that my life included several defining moments, many lessons learned, and an extra dose of just plain good luck.

Was my life worthwhile? Did I make a difference? Yes, my life was worthwhile. Yes, I made a difference. I helped many people, mostly women, achieve their goals and change their lives for the better.

Ronald Reagan frequently said that it was more important to do the right thing than to be concerned about getting credit and recognition for it. I worked quietly and conscientiously behind the scenes for the things I believed in.

I accepted difficult professional challenges to convince myself and other women that it could be done. I helped my colleagues understand and appreciate foreign cultures and traditions. At the same time, I promoted and defended America at every opportunity.

I am proudest of my mentoring style of leadership. It was always a labor of love. I never stayed too long in the top position. I founded a number of enduring and worthwhile women's organizations. When the time was right, I stepped aside and opened the pathway for others to follow.

I regret not having gone to law school or earning a master of business administration (MBA). For women of my generation, law degrees were immediate door openers to high-level positions. It was expensive to pursue postgraduate work. I did not have the resources to do so. On the home front, I wish I could have been a better cook and a more avid sports fan, but there were never enough hours in the day.

My parents would be proud of my career achievements and personal choices. They were always with me—their spirit and love guiding me every step of the way. One thing I know for sure: I stayed on course and never narrowed my horizons. It's hard to know the real impact one has had on one's children, spouse, friends, colleagues, and family members. For my part I tried to inspire my children to set high standards for themselves and pursue their lives with confidence and determination. I also wanted my children to be proud of my life and respect my decisions.

I personally never believed the only purpose of life is to be happy. I wanted to be useful, to be honorable, to be compassionate. Above all, I wanted to matter, to count, to stand for something, to have made some difference to show that I lived at all. I joined the historic march of the Jewish people that began centuries ago. I nurtured the dream my father believed in all his life.

In 2016, Sam and I celebrated our forty-fifth wedding anniversary. Our story is one of love at first sight. It is a story of the triumph of our love for one another and our determination to make it work. It is about a second marriage with his, mine, and our children and grandchildren—a path well-traveled by many other couples. It is a path that can be difficult and demanding.

Sam and I were determined to succeed. Our feelings for one another strengthened as the years went by. As a result of his love for me and support for our unusual commuter lifestyle, demanding careers, and passion for politics, we became lifelong friends, companions, and lovers. Ours is a compelling story of two people who made the choice forty-five years ago to love one other and who never lost sight of their original commitment.

In the end, it's all about family and those you love and those who love you in return. My children and my husband have been my greatest inspiration. They believed in me and my dreams. It has been a remarkable journey for all of us. Thank you for traveling the road with me.

"I swear in the days still left we will walk in fields of gold," sang my favorite singer, the late Eva Cassidy.

Betty Levitt with baby, Phyllis, Montreal, Canada, circa 1937

Julius Levitt (on far right) and resistance fighters, Lithuania, circa 1929

Betty and Julius Levitt, New York, circa 1967

Phyllis in Geneva, Switzerland, on the Mont Blanc Bridge, circa 1960

Phyllis and son David, Monte Carlo, 1969

Phyllis and Sam Kaminsky's wedding, Carlyle Hotel, New York, June 24, 1971

Phyllis's sister, Sharon Roth, and her daughter, Jennifer, circa 1985

Phyllis, David, and Glenn at the White House Fourth of July picnic, 1981

The Avivi family cousins in Israel, circa 2000

Phyllis and Sam, circa 2000

Glenn and David in Israel, circa 1992

Sam and Glenn Kaminsky, circa 2000

David and his father, Janez Hacin, Geneva, Switzerland, circa 2010

Phyllis and Sam, North Lake Tahoe, Nevada, circa 2000

Phyllis's seventieth birthday celebration with Sam,
David, and Glenn, December 2006

David and his partner, Tim Grafft, circa 2000

Phyllis and Sam with David and Tim, Vermont, summer 2006

Phyllis and Sam, Maine, summer of 2015

Phyllis with David and Glenn, circa 2000

Phyllis and Sam forty-five years later

Phyllis with newborn Bella, October 2015

Bella (five months) with Glenn and Toby, 2016

Bella at nine months, 2016

Phyllis and Sam with grandchildren, October 2013

Sam's eightieth birthday party, with all the children, grandchildren, and great-grandchildren, Scottsdale, Arizona, February 2016

Phyllis Kaminsky Timeline

1936–1945	Living in Montreal, Canada
September 1945	Immigration to the United States
1945–1950	Living in Bronx, New York
	Herman Ridder P.S. 98 Junior High School
1950–1953	Living in Long Island City, New York
	William Cullen Bryant High School
1953–1954	Miami University, Oxford, Ohio
1954–1957	University of Michigan, Ann Arbor, Michigan
1956–1957	Internships: US Department of State, US Hungarian Refugee Program
1957–1958	Living in New York City
	Working for Ford Foundation, Foreign Policy Association
1958	School of Public Administration—School of Russian Studies
	Columbia University, New York
May 1958	US citizenship granted
Summer 1958	Trip to Europe
February 1959	Marriage to Janez Hacin, Geneva, Switzerland
1959–1963	Working for United Nations, Chrysler International, McKinsey and Company
July 7, 1961	Birth of son David Janez Hacin
December 1963	Return to New York with David
1964–1967	Grey Advertising, New York
1967–1968	Department of Public Events, City of New York
1968–1970	Monte Carlo, Principality of Monaco
August 1970	Publicist for Harold Robbins Book Tour
September 1970	Return to New York
October 1970	Official Hostess: Mayor's Committee for UN's 25th Anniversary
November 1970	Speaker Coordinator: United Jewish Appeal, New York

Phyllis Kaminsky

November 1970	Met Sam Kaminsky at Holiday Inn, Irwin, Pennsylvania
June 1971	Marriage to Sam, Carlyle Hotel, New York
1971–1980	Living in Johnstown, Pennsylvania
March 28, 1971	Birth of son Glenn Harold Kaminsky
July 20, 1977	Johnstown flood
July 31, 1977	Death of my father, Julius Levitt
1979–1983	Jerusalem Women's Seminar, Egypt and Israel
1980	Reagan-Bush Presidential Campaign and Transition Team
January 21, 1981	Press Officer: the White House, National Security Council
August 1981	Trip to Morocco by invitation of King Hassan
1981	Charter Member: Washington Women's Forum
1982	Presidential Appointment: US Delegate UN Commission on Status of Women, Vienna, Austria
1982–1983	Director, Office of Public Liaison: US Information Agency
July 1983	Trip to Tunisia by invitation of US Ambassador Walter Cutler
1983–1988	Director: UN Information Center, Washington, DC
1984	Official UN Trip: Golan Heights, Sinai, Lebanon, Jerusalem
1986	Official UN Trip: London, Paris, Rome, Moscow, Geneva
1984–1989	Director: International Institute for Women's Political Leadership
March 1989	Established Kaminsky Associates International Consulting Firm
1989–1992	Cofounder and President: International Women's Media Foundation

1989–1993	Board of Directors: International Republican Institute
1990–1992	Presidential Appointment: Board of Visitors, US Air Force Academy
1990–1992	Chair: Official Election Observer Missions to Bosnia, Serbia, Kosovo, Croatia, Slovenia, Macedonia, Montenegro
June 1990	Participated in Official Election Observer Mission to Czechoslovakia
October 24, 1999	Death of my mother, Betty Levitt
July 1992	Trip to Slovenia by invitation of President Milan Kučan
June 1993	Cochair: International Women's Conference, Saint Petersburg, Russia
1994–1996	Board of Directors: Association of Universities for Research in Autonomy
1996–2008	Presidential Appointment: US Commission of America's Heritage Abroad
1997–2001	Board of Directors: Select appointments PLC, London, England
June 26, 1998	Signed US bilateral cultural cooperation treaty with Lithuania
2001–2013	Board of Directors: Leica Geosystems LLC, Atlanta, Georgia
2001–2006	Board of Directors: Vedior NV, Amsterdam, Holland
2002–2015	Board of Directors: Kaba Mas Corporation, Lexington, Kentucky
2002–2008	Presidential Appointment: Board of Visitors, National Defense University
March 2003	Presidential Appointment: US Delegate to UN Human Rights Commission

February 2005	National Defense University: Pentagon Capstone Mission
	Israel, Turkey, Romania, Italy, Germany, Belgium
October 2006	Breast cancer surgery
2003–present	Residence in Scottsdale, Arizona, and Chevy Chase, Maryland

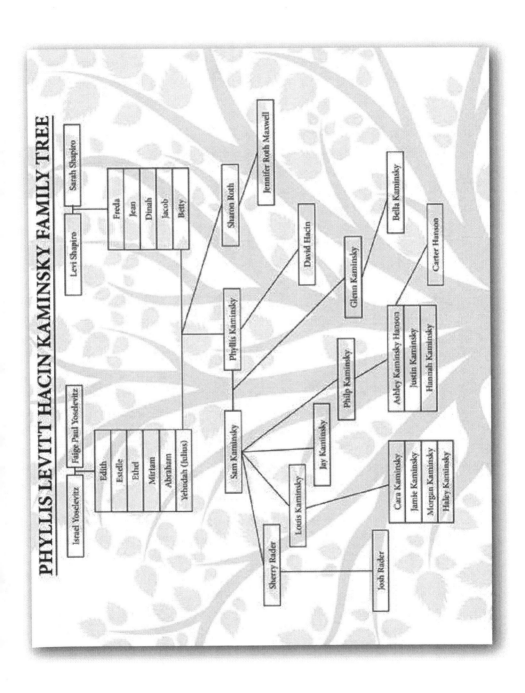

PHYLLIS LEVITT HACIN KAMINSKY FAMILY TREE

End Note
Halifax Where It All Began

On September 10, 2012, Phyllis and Sam Kaminsky arrived at the port of Halifax, Nova Scotia, on board the cruise ship *Norwegian Gem*.

At the immigration records office located at the port, Canadian immigration officials assisted them in finding the following information:

SHIP NAME—LITUANIA/KOSCIUSZKO (Background Information on Ship Included)
Departed Danzig, Poland—January 10, 1930
Arrived Halifax, Nova Scotia—January 22, 1930
ONBOARD and listed on the Ship Manifest:
JULIUS LEVITT—registered as Judelia Joselevitz—age 22—born in Ukmerge, Lithuania—Religion—Hebrew
Profession—Yiddish Teacher—Father—Israel Joselevitz—Ukmerge, Lithuania—Personal Funds—$10.—

    Contact: Sister Edith Kusnitt, 134 Laurier Ave. W, Montreal, Canada—Nationality—Lithuanian

    Listed on Page 4 of the Ship Manifest
BETTY SHAPIRO—registered as Gitl Szapira—age 19—born in Ploskurova, Poland—Religion—Hebrew
Profession—Pupil—Mother—Sara Szapira living in Lvov, Poland—Personal Funds—$6.—

    Contact: Brother Jack Szapira, 5902 Esplanade Avenue, Montreal, Canada—Nationality—Polish
The Last passenger listed on the Ship Manifest entered handwritten.

Betty and Julius disembarked and boarded a Canadian train to start a new life. They were married on September 25, 1931. Phyllis was born on December 1, 1936, and Sharon was born on January 6, 1945.

ADDITIONAL INFORMATION

Bertha (Betty Shapiro) was born in Proskuriv, Russia, on the Polish border. She was raised in Chornoy Ostrov in Poland. Her mother was named Sarah. Her father, Levi, was killed in a pogrom by armed Polish thugs in 1929. She had three sisters, Freda, Dinah, and Jean, and one brother, Jacob. Betty became a naturalized American citizen in 1954 in White Plains, New York. She passed away in Florida on October 24, 1999.

Julius Yoselevitz (later Levitt) was born in Ukmerge (Wilkomir), a suburb of Kaunas, Lithuania (forty-three miles north, near the German border). He graduated from the University of Lithuania in 1926. His mother was named Faige Paul. His father was named Israel. He had four sisters, Edith, Estelle, Ethel, and Miriam. Ethel died in childbirth. He had one brother, Abraham, who was killed in a pogrom. Julius became a naturalized American citizen in 1952. He passed away on July 31, 1977.

Special Acknowledgment

In 2014 I took a course in creative writing taught by Dr. Debra Ann Schwartz of Arizona State University. Debra became my friend. She midwifed this book. She inspired me to write. She gave me a nudge when it looked as if I was slowing down. She gave me the confidence to see it through to the last chapter. The book would not have happened without her constant presence and dedication to the telling of my personal story.

In early May 2016, Debbie went on a hiking trip to Sedona. She was a spiritual and sensual soul who loved the environment and reveled in the beauty and power of nature. Debbie had a terrible accident and tragically died.

I will always remember Debbie, as will the many other students whose lives she changed. I am saddened beyond words that she is gone and will not see the finished product. I will be eternally grateful for her friendship, sensitivity, and extraordinary writing skills.

I grieve with her family—her mother, Audrey, and her younger sister, Sandy. I will never forget her winning smile and her way with words. It was a blessing to have known her for the short time she was part of my life.

I think of her very often and still find myself frequently seeking her advice. This book is a testament to Debbie's amazing life, her rich talent, and her creative vision. She was a beautiful person.

Phyllis Kaminsky
July 2016

Acknowledgments

Special thanks to: my devoted husband and proofreader, Sam Kaminsky; my late congressman, John P. Murtha; my mentor, the late Gordon Zacks; my political mentor, Lee Atwater; my Reagan Administration colleagues, the Honorable Bill Clarke, Ambassador Helene von Damm, the Honorable Nancy Reynolds, the late Ambassador Jeane Kirkpatrick, the Honorable Edwin and Ursula Meese, the Honorable Mae Sue Talley; my defense-industry friends, Dr. Robert Trice, General (ret.) James Jamerson, the Honorable Gordon England, the Honorable Mike Wynne, Captain (ret.) Ron Covais; my Turkish partner and dear friend, Aydan Kodaloglu; and my long-time friend, Mira Ricardel. All of them had confidence in me and opened many doors along the way.

A special thanks to Tim Grafft, our talented family archivist and photographer. Many thanks to my grandson, Justin, for his technology expertise and infinite patience.

And, of course, thank you to my family and friends who encouraged me and waited patiently for this book to be completed.

Made in the USA
Columbia, SC
18 July 2018